A journey of a thousand miles ... ... begins with the first step

Dr. Sundari K

DK's BOOKS FOR ALL

(an imprint of Low Price Publications)
Delhi-110052

First Published 2012
Revised Edition 2019

ISBN 13: 978-81-7386-273-1
ISBN 10: 81-7386-273-7

Published By
DK's BOOKS FOR ALL
(an imprint of Low Price Publications)
A-6, Second Floor, Nimri Commercial Centre,
Ashok Vihar Phase-4, Delhi - 110 052
Tel.: +91 11 4706 1936
website: www.Lppindia.com
e-mail: info@Lppindia.com

Printed At
D K Fine Art Press P Ltd.
Delhi-110052

PRINTED IN INDIA

In memory of my parents

Tranquebar Viswanath Iyer (1905-1975)

and V Jayalaxmi (1916-1986)

Preface

"A journey of a thousand miles begins with the first step," is a Chinese proverb which I thought best captures, the spirit and philosophy of the process of education. It is not merely a single step, but the first step that sets one going on a journey. Taking that first step is often difficult but, once this crucial step is taken, the journey has begun and the rest follows. Hence, the title of this book, reflects the critical nature of the first step in any journey.

Traveling through many roads, as a student and then as a teacher, I found that every step can be enriching. The activities and tasks, that are necessary for transforming externally available information into internal knowledge and wisdom become a lifelong asset if one takes the time and effort. From my many teachers I absorbed the tools and techniques of a variety of disciplines. Yet, it is through transmitting these to students, through several decades, that I assimilated the nuances of the happenings within the human personality that makes education a lifelong journey of discovery.

The book is structured around the story of a boy named 'Prithvi', who is representative of people, both young and old, male and female, who tread the paths of education in different places and different times. Prithvi's struggle and motivation to learn amidst the odds encountered are narrated in Unit A. The Unit B that follows the narration, contains topics pertinent to the narration. Motivation and other topics, with tips and techniques to keep the fire burning within, to have the patience and persistence to continue the daily process of education are dealt with. This story telling style of introducing concepts has been adopted throughout the book. It has been found effective in capturing and retaining the interest and attention of individuals in the numerous training programs and classes conducted in academic settings–classrooms and community settings–hospitals, village self help groups and non-governmental organizations. Tho concept and style has been honed and tried on numerous students in the four decades of pedagogy.

The book begins with 'Prithvi' passing his plus two exams, but he is in a predicament as he wants to study further but his family could not afford his college education. Unit 1 and 2 describe his motivation and drive from within to excel. He takes up a job as a computer assistant, referred by his neighbor 'Mithra', an archetypal friend, philosopher and guide.

Unit 3 is a discussion on how 'Prithvi' deals with anger and tackles stress and tension, once he begins working. He learns to deal with these emotions, by meditation, morning walks and exercises that his neighbor 'Mithra' taught him.

Unit 4 is about time management or the lack of it in 'Prithvi's' routine of getting ready to work. He finds himself always harried and stressed for time, in spite of getting up early. He takes 'Mithra's' advice and becomes more organized at work and comes up with his time manager.

In Unit 5 the proprietor of the computer institute, observes 'Prithvi's' enthusiasm to learn, and helpful nature when students get stuck in the labs. He decides to give 'Prithvi' the opportunity to take a course and do the practice sessions in the spare time at work. 'Prithvi' thus attends his first lecture and has a hard time concentrating, on his lectures as also with his reading assignments at home. He learns how to improve his concentration.

Unit 6 is about the instructors advice to 'Prithvi' on listening. He learns the difference between just hearing and active listening.

In Unit 7 he learns of the tips and techniques of note-taking. His friend and classmate 'Manasa' helps him to learns the process of taking notes during lectures.

'Prithvi' learns of the tricks in creating associations and mnemonics to convert short-term memory to long-term memory in Unit 8.

In Unit 9 'Manasa' helps 'Prithvi' to see the things he reads in his text, in context, and he learns how to read effectively.

'Prithvi' has to compile a project report for his course; he takes up the challenge to fix the antiquated software program that their institute uses to generate mark statements. He fixes the program and finishes the report in Unit 10. The instructors congratulate him on his hard work, and the proprietor asks him to present his report to the administrative staff, to enable them to make use of the software.

'Prithvi' meets 'Manasa's' parents and shares his anxiety about the impending presentation. Her father talks of his high school and college experiences as a compere for the cultural show. 'Prithvi' realizes that he is not alone in his dread, for speaking in public in Unit 11. He prepares well and gives an excellent presentation.

In Unit 12 'Prithvi' prepares for his final exam. He learns of the different types of tests, and the objectives of testing. He prepares well for the test and gets the job of junior lecturer in the institute.

The above 12 units have been organized around the challenges that any young professional or student like 'Prithvi' would face in today's world. The journey of 'Prithvi' began with the first step he took and so his life's journey took a completely different route. Valuable insights, tips and techniques to excel amidst these obstacles and distractions, are also provided. Your suggestions, ideas and feedback are always welcome. Please e-mail me at **sundarikrishnamurthy@gmail.com**. My other forthcoming books are: "India –Beyond Curry, Caste and Cow", "Communication: A Process and Product of Society", "Health Communication: Interpersonal, Group and Organizational Communication in Health Settings", and "Logic: The Processes of Reasoning".

K Sundari
Chennai, India
5 April, 2019

Contents

About the Author

Sundari Krishnamurthy was the Academic Dean (2005 to 2007) and Chair of the Department of Public Relations (from 2006) at Stella Maris College (Autonomous) Chennai, India in which college she has been a career academic for over four decades.

She is an active academician, who has presented over 170 papers, articles and presentations in numerous national and international conferences; guided thesis research at various levels including doctoral students; involved in the design of new courses and curriculum development, and served in various advisory committees. She was the Fulbright *Scholar in Residence* for the year 2000-01, at the Hillsborough Community College, Tampa, U.S.A, where she designed, developed and taught a semester-long Asian Humanities course. She has guest lectured and served as consultant, in various institutions, both national and international and has developed and taught innovative courses in philosophy, logic, communication and public relations.

As a social scientist, she has spearheaded numerous case studies developmental projects and training programs. The social impact of technology namely Internet, in the villages of south India, field surveys of local fishing and tribal communities, study of air pollution and water management, empowerment of women and communication media in India are some of the challenging projects undertaken by her.

She is a lifetime member of a number of prestigious organizations including, Madras Philosophy Society, Madras Psychology Society, Indian Society of Health Administrators, Indian Society for Training and Development and also a member of International Communication Association and FICCI Ladies Organization. Apart from playing an active role in the above-mentioned organizations, she was the Item Writer and Expert Member for the Tamil Nadu Public Service Commission (1978-84), Union Public Service Commission (1980-86) and Staff Selection Commission (1993-1999). These are a sample of the many positions held by Dr. Sundari in her four decades of being a proactive educationist, innovative trainer and researcher. She was Director of the Centre for Networking and Communications (2013-2019) in which she executed outreach programs with Chambers of Commerce, N.G.O's, Corporate CSR departments and Government departments like KVIC, CPPPI, C.S.C. e-governance, National Literacy Mission and PMGDISHA. She is listed in Reference Asia: Asia's Who's Who of Men and Women of Achievement, FICCI Ladies Organization Directory and Trainers and Training Institutions, Directory of ISTD, India.

Dr. Sundari is married to Krishnamurthy, a (retired) bureaucrat. She has two sons, Ashok – a cardiologist and Narayanan, a neuroscientist. The Krishnamurthy's have a grandson, Akshay Sundar and grand-daughter, Shriya and a daughter-in-law, Subha- a radiologist.

"HE LIVED WITH HIS FATHER AND MOTHER IN A TENEMENT CLOSE TO THE BEACH"

Unit 1 A

Prithvi makes the decision

Keywords

1. Motivation	3. Self-esteem	5. Self-image
2. Positive attitude	4. Confidence	6. Values

Read this narrative about a boy like you who became successful in life due to his persistent effort and intelligence.

Prithvi was a laborer's son. He lived with his father and mother in a tenement close to the beach. There were several buildings of three to four floors consisting of one-roomed apartments, constructed by the government for which they charged a meager rent. His father had to work all day to earn money, which was just about enough to cater to the basic necessities of life. But Prithvi did not want to become a laborer like his father. When he completed his schooling, he told his father, "You have been a laborer all your life. So was your father, his father and grandfather. I want to be different. I want to be successful in life."

"How is that possible?" his father asked him, "This is our karma, our destiny. We can't do anything about it."

"No, that is not true. I think that if I try hard enough I can bring about a change in our life-style."

"But, what about the money, Prithvi? We hardly have enough money for two meals a day. Where can I get the money for your education?"

"Don't worry about the money. I think that if I try, I will be able to work and earn the money required to pay my fees."

"I wish I could fulfill your dreams. But, I am so helpless."

"I can tell you one thing." His mother said, "You need not give the money you earn to the family. I will manage the house with the money your father brings home for some more time."

Now that he had decided as to what he wanted to do, Prithvi was determined to come up in life. However, he had no sense of direction as to where to go or whom to approach.

Prithvi joined his friends as they gathered around their favorite spot where they smoked and chatted about movies and girls. Most of them had failed in their Plus Two exams, but did not seem to be bothered about it. And when he told them about his aspirations, they laughed at him.

"Prithvi, you are just confused. Here, take this cigarette. You will feel better after you smoke. What you are saying can happen only in the movies. Be practical like us. We have already started working for Rudra and we are getting a lot of money everyday. We have seen all the latest movies and we are having fun. Forget all of this. Let us go to a bar and enjoy ourselves. Tomorrow, I will take you to Rudra and he will give you a job."

Prithvi accepted the cigarette, but did not feel like joining them for the night, though he was tempted. He wanted a clear mind to do some serious thinking. He knew the kind of job he would have to do for Rudra. He was a powerful man in the locality. Even the police did not dare to interfere with him. He did not want to work for him. How was he going to earn money? How was he to get a job? He had to begin somewhere.

Self-appraisal

Answer these questions:

1. Do you think that Prithvi's decision is right ? Will he be successful?
2. What is motivation?

"CAME OUT FOR A WALK ?" MITHRA ASKED HIM

Unit 1 B

The Key to Success

"*I find that the harder I work, the more luck I seem to have.*" —*Thomas Jefferson* (1743-1826)

1.1 Motivation – the drive from within to achieve

Motivation has to come from within. The urge to learn, to understand and to get to know things will surely lead an individual to success.

1.2 Self-image and Self-esteem

Self-image is the picture you have of yourself in your mind. Self-esteem is the calculation of your own worth, your sense of worthiness you have in your mind. If your self-image is positive and your self-esteem is high, you achieve the targets and goals you have set for yourself in life.

When learning in a group, individuals may have come from different backgrounds. Some may have had opportunities, which others may not have had them. If the learner's self-image and self-esteem are positive, he is sure to learn faster and better than an individual who has no confidence in himself.

1.3 How to maintain a good sense of self-image and self-esteem

To maintain healthy sense of esteem you must:

1.3.1 Celebrate your strengths and achievements

1.3.2 Work smarter, not just harder

Set targets which are

- **S**pecific
- **M**easurable
- **A**ttainable
- **R**ealistic
- **T**ime bound

1.3.3 Do not measure yourself against unreasonable standards

1.3.4 Try to overcome your weaknesses

Cursing yourself for your weaknesses would be self-defeating. Excessive self-esteem makes a person domineering, while a person with low self-esteem is too self-effacing. The right balance between the two has to be attained.

Unit 2 A

Prithvi's Dis-ease

Keywords

1. Past experience	3. Pride in work	5. Inhibit
2. Job satisfaction	4. Confidence	6. Enrich

The heat of the summer was stifling. Prithvi decided to go for a small stroll. He started walking towards the small shop that was open till late in the night. Mithra was there too. Mithra lived alone in a small flat beside his tenement. He had retired after thirty-eight years of service as an assistant in a General Hospital.

He never spoke to anyone in the neighborhood, and was something of an introvert. When he first moved into the slum five years ago, everyone looked at the move with distrust. He was a loner. He did not have a family. He cooked food himself, washed his own clothes, washed vessels and swept the house. A woman's job! He was fair, not very tall, with deep set eyes that were alluring. He was different, he was an outsider. Much to their consternation, people had to go to him for help. Whenever their children fell sick or they became unwell, he was able to cure them with herbs he grew on his terrace. Of course, they expected him to give tablets, since he had worked in a hospital.

Anyway, they found him useful as they could not afford to spend the kind of consultation fees that doctors charged. And his methods worked! Prithvi held a sense of grudging respect for this man. He had developed a kind of relationship with him over the years, which was non-verbal. He wanted to prove something to his man. He would have liked to speak to him, but for the fear that people may label him queer for associating himself with such a person.

"Came out for a walk?" Mithra asked him.

"Yes. The heat in my house was too much."

"So, how did you do in your Plus Two exams? You received your marks today, didn't you? I saw you go with your classmates to school this morning."

"I got about seventy percent."

"But that's a good score, Why are you so dull?"

"What's the use? I can't afford to go to college. I don't want to be a coolie like my father. I don't want to work for Rudra like my friends. I would like to be different. I don't know what to do..."

"You are confused. I can quite understand. Well, I cannot do anything for you at the moment. But, there is a job available. You may not like it. You have to work as an assistant in a computer shop. Would you be prepared for that kind of a job? You have done your Plus Two and have scored quite well. Would you consider it beneath your sense of dignity to take up such a job."

"Not at all. Let me at least start something. I will take up this work."

"Are you sure you will be able to take it up? There is no point if you have made this decision on the spur of the moment and then decide to quit after a week's work. Think it over tonight and get back to me tomorrow in the morning."

Prithvi met the proprietor of the firm the following morning. His job was to maintain the computer room in good condition. He had to wipe the computers, switch them on in the mornings before the students came to class, set up the overhead projector, distribute hand-outs and the like.

He had to a lot of odd chores for the owner as well. He was sent to pay the electricity bills, the telephone bills and buy vegetables and ration. Prithvi felt frustrated. All that was not his job. He had been hired to work at the shop, not for his proprietor's personal work. Prithvi started to feel tired and hungry towards the evening. The food he carried was insubstantial to sustain him for the whole day.

As he saw the students work with the machines, he felt a twinge of jealousy pass through him. They seemed to brim with confidence and pride. They were educated in good convent schools and spoke to each other in English in a refined manner. They came in bikes or drove cars and wore the best of clothes. He looked around the room. The cool air-conditioned room with the sleek furniture and bright lights was such a contrast to the home he had to go back to at the end of the day.

Was all the trouble he was undergoing worth what he was going to achieve in the end? Should he quit? Something stopped Prithvi from leaving his job. It was his fascination for computers. He had come to think of the lab as his own. He looked with pride at the lab. Not even a speck of dust could be seen. It gave him immense satisfaction to see the white tiled floors sparkle with cleanliness. He resolved to stay firm in his decision. He made his choice and now there was no turning back.

Self-appraisal

Answer these questions:

1. If a student is not confident, do you think he will be successful?
2. What is self-esteem?
3. When a student meets with failure in his endeavors, what should he do?

Unit 2 B

Past Experience

"Two roads diverged in a wood, and I took the one less traveled by and that has made all the difference!"

—Robert Frost

The Road Not Taken

2.1 The influence of the past on the present

Past experience in learning, for a person may have been good or bad. Bad experiences in the past should never deter a person from achieving his goal. Similarly, a good experience in the past or knowledge of the subject or skill in a job, must be related to present learning or work situation.

In the learning process, the individual's mind has to be open to new learning. He may even have to 'unlearn' what he had learnt in the past. For instance, a person who is used to learning by rote will find it difficult to understand a concept and then learn, as he is not accustomed to such a method.

Each individual learns differently and at different speeds. An individual should not feel stressed that he is faster or slower than others in his group.

Each person may have different motives for having chosen a course of study or occupation. It may be due to compulsion, or a conscious choice. But the important thing is that if a person does not get what he likes, he should learn to like what he has got. There are moments in life when certain irrevocable decisions have to be taken. Once the decision has been made, there is no point in thinking about the possibilities of the past.

2.2 The need for confidence

Confidence in one's power to achieve; it is integral to the learning process. The goal to be attained may seem unobtainable, the path intractable and the methods indeterminable. But, anything can be achieved with time and practice.

Unit 3 A

Prithvi's Anger

Keywords

1. Stress	3. Eustress	5. Relaxation
2. Tension	4. Distress	6. Paranoia

As Prithvi reached home in the evening, he felt a wave of anger sweep over him. He looked at the slum tenement that he had been born and brought up in, and had lived all his life. He noticed the dirt and garbage by the sides of the road. A woman was washing clothes and the water flowed on the road. Water stood stagnated on the street, like a cesspool. The meat and fish at the butcher's lay molding by the sides of the road. It was just abominable.

Was this the same road he had played marbles as a boy? He had grown up in such filth and dirt? He had never noticed all this earlier, the squalor and the dirt seemed to scream at him. He felt nauseated as he inhaled the air around him.

HE SET ABOUT CLEANING THE HOUSE

He entered his house and saw how squalid it was. The floor was dull with dirt. Dust had settled everywhere and lay like a film on all the things. Cobwebs hung from the ceiling. The surge of anger rushed at him again. He set about cleaning the house. He ransacked his cupboard and threw away all wallets, posters of film-stars and cricket-stars carefully cut from magazines, quills, shells, labels, film strips, tops, stones and marbles – all that was worthless trash! He felt a sense of freedom as he threw it all away. Why on earth had he channeled all his energy towards something like this?

He dusted the room and removed the cobwebs. He scrubbed the floor with all the force he could muster, and washed it until it seemed thoroughly clean. The house looked better and brighter at the end of it all. He was surprised that he was not as angry as he had been a few hours ago. Instead of feeling tired, he felt renewed with energy. He smiled at his mother who gave him his black coffee with a bewildered look.

He shared with her his experience during the day, his hopes, his fears, his anxieties and misgivings, as he helped her roll the roti for dinner. He felt a lot better after talking to her. Instead of joining his friends as usual, he went to the terrace from where he could see the beach. People looked like tiny ants moving on the sand. Cars, bikes and buses which looked huge at the eye level, looked like toys as they rushed past the road. The anger and frustration he had felt earlier in the evening that seemed so magnified, was now as diminished as those cars. The sun set gloriously against the sea. Prithvi felt relaxed and was prepared to meet another day.

Self-appraisal

Answer these questions:

1. Why does Prithvi feel angry when he looks at the environment he lives in?
2. Why didn't Prithvi notice the unclean surroundings before?
3. Why doesn't Prithvi feel angry after cleaning his house?

Unit 3 B

How to Tackle Tension?

"A pessimist sees the difficulty in every opportunity: an optimist sees the opportunity in every difficulty."

—Sir Winston Churchill (1874-1965)

3.1 Tension—a problem that has a solution

Stress or tension is a part of our life. In fact, if there were no stress, if there was no pressure, or the drive for man to achieve. And to compete, we would still be in the caves instead of contemplating about colonies on the moon. We would sink into ennui or boredom and life would become meaningless.

We need stress, that is eustress, but not too much stress or distress. Eustress keeps us alert, motivates us to face challenges and drives us to solve problems. This type of stress is manageable and even necessary. Distress, on the other hand, occurs when the body reacts to a particular situation as though it were a life or death issue. The feeling you experience the moment before you enter the examination hall or the moment before you wait to talk to the head of your department or the moment before you enter the interview hall are examples of distress. What is required is a more realistic and reasonable approach.

Stress or tension could be caused due to various reasons – physical, mental or social. Everything in this world has a cause and an effect. Tension or stress is the product of some cause. If the cause is detected and treated, a person can be relieved of stress.

3.2 Tension can be tackled in several ways

3.2.1 Talk to someone

A person under stress will find it useful to talk to friends or the family about his worries.

3.2.2 Divert your energy from the sources of stress

One could try to direct one's anger or frustration by doing work, meditation or exercise. It is important that the senses are kept under the control of the mind. The mind or the intellect is like a charioteer who has to harness the five horses (the senses) to *Buddhi* or *Viveka* in the journey of life. The mind is a powerful weapon, unlike the senses which are passive and receptive. However, the mind is an easy prey to temptation. It is a receptacle of both the good and the bad, and it is very often difficult to forget what is bad or unnecessary. Tension is caused because the mind is left to wander and the person looses control. Meditation or exercise done on a regular basis helps a student control his mind.

3.2.3 Help others

Helping others and being of service to people who are more needy than one's self, gives a person great joy and satisfaction.

3.2.4 Divide work into parts

At a point of time, it may seem that there are too many things to be done. The work to be completed may seem unending and immense. However, if the work is divided into manageable parts or segments, it can be completed within the scheduled time. A journey of a thousand miles begins with a single step. Take up one thing at a time, give it full attention and complete it thoroughly.

3.2.5 Relaxation methods

Relaxation for sufficient periods of time is important too. Relaxation does not mean that a person has to sleep for long hours. It just means that he has to engage himself in some activity that interests him other than his regular work. Good music, reading books, a work out or quick game with a friend, practicing yoga or even conversing with elders are possible forms of relaxation.

MITHRA WAS EXERCISING

Unit 4 A

Prithvi Fights with Time

Keywords

1. Time management	3. Schedule	5. Prioritize
2. Checklist	4. Allocate	6. Organize

Prithvi woke up early in the morning. It was not out of habit, but for the fact that the shirt he had to wear was a little damp, and had to be dried in the morning sun. He took his shirt to the terrace and clipped it on to the clothes-line. Prithvi noticed someone on the neighboring terrace, Mithra was exercising. Prithvi was surprised, to see old Mithra exercising at his age. He wondered if Mithra would get tired after so much of strain, as he waited impatiently for his shirt to dry. He only had five good shirts that he wore through the week. They were all dirty now and needed to be washed, and it was getting late!

Prithvi darted down the stairs in a great hurry. He looked at the clock. Six-thirty ! He put on his shirt with one hand as he tried to comb his hair with the other. He could not find his watch. He searched for it high and low. After a desperate hunt for ten minutes, he found it amongst his clothes. He had thrown it casually the previous evening after the whole day's work. He couldn't find his lunch box. After a search for five minutes, he remembered that he had not left it out for his mother to wash the previous evening. He found it in his bag. Now, he had to wash it before he could pack lunch. It was getting late! He decided to skip breakfast. He didn't have the time! He hastened to the bus stop. His bus had gone already. He was late!

However much he tried every day to reach his office early, he just reached there on time. By the time he arrived at the office, it was eight o'clock. The students would start coming in by eight-fifteen! He switched on the computers as he wiped them hurriedly. He checked the time table and found that it was the teacher who always used the OHP. He set it up in a hurry. The light wouldn't focus correctly. The students started coming in. Why did this happen today? He had in fact got up earlier than usual. He simply did not seem to have the time. The day before, he had come to the bus stop on time, but had to go back home to pick up his lunch-box that he had forgotten. The other day, it was his wallet. There must be a simpler way out, Prithvi thought, as he walked down his street that evening.

Self Appraisal

Answer these questions:

1. What is Prithvi's idea about exercising?
2. Why do you think Prithvi is always late to the office?
3. How can Prithvi manage his time?

Unit 4 B

Using Time Effectively

"Fill the unforgiving minute with sixty seconds worth of distance run." —*Rudyard Kipling (1865-1936)*

4.1 Time management tactics

Time is a very important and useful resource. But paradoxically, it is irretrievable. The wheels of time ever move forward, and a minute lost can never be regained. With careful planning and practice, you can learn to manage time effectively. Planning time does not mean following a rigorous military-like schedule. Rather, it is a means of making intelligent decisions about when it is the easiest and most efficient to get work done. Time management is the art of working smarter, not just harder, and a good time manager is the key.

4.1.1 Step one: Prepare a checklist

You must first be aware of all the things that have to be done. So, make a checklist of all the things to be done at a certain point of time. You could call this your time manager, a manager who helps you to organize your work based on the time available.

4.1.1.1 Writing a checklist is helpful in two ways

a) in planning

b) in greater productivity

Time is difficult to understand, and master. It is relative, at times slow, at times fast. In the beginning of the academic year, there seems to be a lot of time. But, towards the end of the year, as exams start nearing, there seems to be no time.

4.1.1.2 Writing a checklist is very helpful in other ways too

a) It gives you a realistic idea of the actual time available and the amount of work to be done within that time.

b) All the work to be done big or small will be written. So, you will never forget a pending task.

c) You will have a short-term view and a long-term view of the work to be done.

d) You can organize work according to their urgency or need.

4.1.1.3 How to prepare a checklist

Make a list of study-related tasks to be done. This is a method you may be following already. You may have a calendar where you note down the important dates of tests and assignments. This has to be just organized in terms of the number of classes for each paper, the assignments to be submitted and their deadlines, the tests in those subjects with the dates, the number of classes of lab practice and the amount of reading to be done. The only difference between a calendar and this is that, this checklist has to be reviewed every week and that, it includes all aspects of your study.

4.1.2 Step Two: Make an estimate of the time required

After preparing the checklist, estimate the amount of time each task will consume and record it beside each task. This may initially not be accurate. In fact, you may find that you had allotted either too much or too little time for a job. But, with practice, this will improve. Each work can be broken into parts, and the time can be allotted. An assignment or project work can be divided like this:

Tasks	Time estimated
1) To select the topic and getting approval from the teacher	1hr
2) To do bibliographic research in the library and check on material available on the topic	1hr
3) To work in the library	5hr
4) To organize library notes, categorize the material and prepare an outline	1hr to 4hr
5) To write the rough copy	3hr
6) To revise, edit and write the fair copy	3hr
7) To type the fair copy	3hr
Total number of hours required to write the assignment	17hr
Safety margin	3hr
Total number of hours required	20hr

A safety margin has to be added to this total, in case there has been an underestimation of time at some point or an emergency situation arises (the library may not open when you are free, the book you require may not be available in the library, there may be power failure when you decide to write, or you might have guests at home, or the typist who keys in may delay the work).

The next step is to divide the total by the number of weeks you have to do the assignment. For example:

Time estimated to do the assignment	:	20 hr
Number of weeks available	:	5 weeks
Amount of work per week	:	4 hr per week

This would mean that four hours of work have to be allotted in your time manager for the assignment for the next five weeks. Although, the time estimated may be wild guesses initially, you will improve with practice. This exercise gives you a realistic picture of the actual time you have to do a task.

4.1.3 Step Three: Setting priority

The next step is to prioritize the tasks based on their importance, number the tasks on hand, and then rank them in order. This may depend on several criteria like marks, due dates and so on. Setting priority forces you to weigh the importance of each item on the task list, and to make a conscious, thoughtful decision about what to do and when it should be done. Once the time plan has been created, following the steps is easy, and each item may be crossed out of the list when it is finished.

4.1.4 Step Four: Follow the plan

The purpose of a time schedule is not to make a slave of the individual, but to handle scholastic inefficiency and noncommittal anxiety. There are several things to remember, even after the checklist has been made and tasks prioritized, which have to be considered when you start to execute the plan.

4.1.4.1 Persistence pays off

The whole process becomes successful only when the plan is monitored, analyzed and reviewed from time to time until it works. One of the important things to keep in mind while planning time is that it takes time to practice and polish this method. One of the reasons why students give up a time plan is that they assume that once a time plan is drawn up, everything is over. Some frustration is inevitable and even to be expected. Patience is a virtue that helps to work the plan through trial and error, and constant fine-tuning and adjustments to the schedule.

4.1.4.2 Discipline saves time

There is no one but you to monitor how effectively you are using time available. Some time has to be set aside everyday to check as to how the time-plan is working. If certain tasks are yet to be completed, find out why they had slipped the schedule. An analysis of how or why a time-plan does not work is the key to successful self-monitoring.

4.1.4.3 Change aids time-plan

Flexibility is an important part of time-plan. If, for instance, two hours have been allotted to work on an assignment, and thoughts seem to flow fluently, do not stop when the stipulated two hour ends. Continue to work on the assignment. Find out negative patterns that may emerge and analyze their source. Flexibility to make adjustments in the plan, and expecting the unexpected will lead to a successful time-plan.

4.1.4.4 System steadies

As far as possible, schedule the time slots for study at the same time everyday, to inculcate a systematic and habitual approach to studies.

4.1.4.5 Creativity helps

Free time should be used effectively. The hours between classes are the most misused time by students. This time can be used for reviewing the notes of the previous class or for preparing for the next class. The bigger your repertoire of time managing strategies, the greater your chances of success as a student. If you can manage time in the stressful environment of studies, then you can be confident of managing time in any situation after graduation. It is a skill that you will benefit from for life. The work habits of many people who have achieved outstanding careers show an effective and well-designed pattern of time management.

Your time manager

Name : ______________________

Month : ______________________

From : ______________________

To : ______________________

Forenoon

Time	Day 1 Date	Day 2 Date	Day 3 Date	Day 4 Date	Day 5 Date	Day 6 Date
5:30-6:00						
6:00-6:30						
6:30-7:00						
7:00-7:30						
7:30-8:00						
8:00-8:30						
8:30-9:00						
9:00-9:30						
9:30-10:00						
10:00-10:30						
10:30-11:00						
11:00-11:30						
11:30-12:00						

Afternoon

Time	Day 1 Date	Day 2 Date	Day 3 Date	Day 4 Date	Day 5 Date	Day 6 Date
12:00-12:30						
12:30-1:00						
1:00-1:30						
1:30-2:00						
2:00-2:30						
2:30-3:00						
3:00-3:30						
3:30-4:00						
4:00-4:30						
4:30-5:00						

Evening

Time	Day 1 Date	Day 2 Date	Day 3 Date	Day 4 Date	Day 5 Date	Day 6 Date
5:00-5:30						
5:30-6:00						
6:00-6:30						
6:30-7:00						
7:00-7:30						
7:30-8:00						
8:00-8:30						
8:30-9:00						
9:00-9:30						
9:30-10:00						
10:00-10:30						
10:30-11:00						
11:00-11:30						
11:30-12:00						

A checklist on how you spend your time

After using the time manager for a week fill up this inventory to take stock of how your time has been spent:

Activity		Number of hours spent		Percentage of time the activity occupies	
		Before[1]	After[2]	Before[1]	After[2]
1.	Studying				
2.	Eating				
3.	Sleeping				
4.	Dressing				
5.	Recreation				
6.	Classes & Labs				
7.	Physical activity				
8.	Household work				
9.	Time spent with friends				
10.	Free time				

1 Before using the time manager

2 After using the time manager

"PRITHVI YOU HAVE CHANGED TOTALLY..."

Unit 5 A

Prithvi's Avocation Becomes Vocation

Key words

1. Concentration	4. Physical fatigue
2. Internal distraction	5. Mental fatigue
3. External distraction	6. Study environment

As Prithvi walked home that evening, he kept wondering if there was a way out to prevent all the hustle and bustle and the stress of the mornings. He waved towards his friends who stood by their favorite corner. They did not respond. He wondered if they hadn't noticed him. He waved again. No response. He came closer to them bubbling with enthusiasm to talk to them. He had not seen them for a long time. He was caught up in a busy schedule. He came home late in the evening and was tired to meet them at eleven in the night, their usual time. "Hello," he said, "how are you all? It's a long time since we met."

"Why are you wasting your time with us Prithvi? You have become a very busy person, you don't even have time for us," said one friend.

"Prithvi, you have changed totally. You dress differently. You speak differently. We don't want your condescending 'Hello.." said another.

"Even last week I saw you in the morning going to the bus stop. I waved at you, but, you didn't even acknowledge my presence," said one.

"Wait" said Prithvi "you see I come back home so tired that I cannot even step out of the house. And you, I didn't ignore you deliberately as you seem to think, I was in a tearing hurry because I was late to the office."

"Don't lie Prithvi. You are too tired to meet us. But you seem to meet that old man everday. You know we don't like him. How can you go speak to him."

Prithvi could not convince his friends, much as he tried their conversation only ended in a heated argument.

That evening when he met Mithra, he was too upset. Mithra was very perceptive. He waited for Prithvi to speak.

"Is there no way out?", Prithvi asked.

"Out of what?"

"How much ever early I try to get ready in the mornings, I am always delayed. It has been six months since I started working in this office, and I seem to reach just on time, however much I try. It's a battle everyday."

"Prithvi, your problem is in bad planning and mis-management of time. You get up early, yes, but you are not organized. There must be a system in everything we do, a method in our madness. Once you create a system, it can be followed easily. It is a question of time. With a little practice, you will fall into the framework of the system." Mithra suggested several ideas to Prithvi to organize his time.

It took Prithvi nearly two months to perfect the system Mithra taught him. He now had time for other things. He could reach his work on time. Since he had everything ready for each class. He could even listen to the instructors as they taught. He could not understand most of what they lectured, but, whenever he had free time, he began to explore the machines. He could remember most of what they said in the course, because he listened to the same lecture atleast four times in the morning conducted for different batches of students. He tried to do whatever the instructors taught. He became fascinated with computers. He felt he had wasted the six months he had been working there. If only he had listened to the instructors earlier he could have learnt more. This was quite an opportunity.

Prithvi woke up very early that morning. He walked up the beach for his regular exercises. Mithra had taught him a few exercises and yoga. Prithvi felt especially fresh after his sessions of *pranayama*. He had even quit smoking. Of course, it had been difficult, but now the air that he inhaled seemed fresher and invigorating. Even the food that he ate tasted better after he quit chewing *pan.* He watched the sunrise as he walked back home to get ready for work.

He reached the office early, to spend a few uninterrupted minutes with the computer. The students started coming in. It was about 11.30 a.m. The proprietor came for his usual rounds. He watched Prithvi helping out a student who evidently had some problem with the work he was doing. The instructor was at the other end of the room clarifying doubts of seven or eight students who were around him. He had frequently noticed that Prithvi was able to help the students whenever they fumbled over a problem. He was amazed at the motivation of this boy. He remembered how he had come a year ago and how nervous he was at the interview. He had changed a lot. Why not give him a chance? After all he was making a good profit.

Prithvi walked with great joy that evening. Life seemed to take on a glorious hue. He couldn't wait to tell the news to Mithra, who was very happy indeed. " You are luckier than Ekalavya," he said," you have instructors who will teach you."

Prithvi had been offered an intensive course on Windows for a duration of three months. He had to prove his worth in the exams at the end of the course. He had very little time though. It was a formidable task.

Prithvi set out to work immediately. Frequently, he had to do a lot of self-study. He also had difficulty understanding English. He did not understand most of what the instructors said. He had to sit up late in the nights to internalize what he had learnt. This was not an easy task. He was hungry on most days. The dinner he had at 8.00 in the evening was not sufficient to sustain him as he continued working in the late hours of the night. He had to get up early in the mornings.

Besides, he could use the computers only when all his work for the day was over or intermittent breaks when he was free. Everyday, it was an ordeal. The place he lived was not in the least conducive to the kind of aspirations he held. At the moment, there was a festival in the local temple. The whole place bustled with frenetic activity. The loudspeaker was on. Shops had been set up by the roadside, and each hawker was trying to outsmart the other. The ice-cream seller, the sugar candy seller, the sweet seller and the fruit seller were vying with each other to sell their wares. Children were playing at the merry-go-round. Prithvi could not concentrate, the noise was too much.

The police from the local police station came by. They wanted them to clear the shops because they had not got the permission from the concerned authorities. Soon there was a big commotion. A year ago Prithvi would have been a part of all this along with his friends. He would have stood with the other men and watched with vehemence the altercation between them and the police. Now, all he wanted was some peace and quiet.

His friends called him to join them. He closed the doors and all the windows. The noise seeped through. He refused and decided to go to the terrace. The noise was a little subdued. But it was there. Prithvi felt defeated.

He was tired and hungry. There was so much to study and so little time. He would not get another opportunity. If he could prove his worth just this once, he may be allowed to do another course. His whole future could change.

Self-appraisal

1. Why are Prithvi's friends angry with him?
2. Why does Mithra wait for Prithvi to talk first?
3. What is your opinion about the proprietor?
4. Why cannot Prithvi concentrate and study?
5. When you sit down to study, what are the problems you face?

Unit 5 B

Concentration—A Tool to Sharpen the Intellect

"Obstacles are those frightful things you see when you take your eyes off your goal"

—Henry Ford (1863-1947)

5.1 Concentration—the right frame of mind

Concentration is the ability to pay attention to the work on hand, whether it is listening to a lecture, or participation in a discussion, working on an assignment or doing a test. When your powers of concentration are at the highest you will be able to do a greater amount of work.

Here are some techniques to improve your concentration:

5.1.1 Make the place of study a constant

Make it a habit to study in the same place. Select a particular place for study. It could be the corner-most table in the library, your terrace or your study table at home. The study place should be the same everyday, so much so that when you enter that particular niche in the world you get to work automatically.

5.1.2 Internal Distractions

Breaks in concentration occur due to internal distractions – your thoughts wander, you start day dreaming, you start worrying about your personal problems, you start worrying about the whole list of tasks to be done or think about some other thing than the subject you are attempting to study. If this happens frequently, try to change the place of study. If not, change the time of study.

5.1.3 External Distractions

Breaks in concentration occur due to external distractions too. Make it clear to the rest of the world (your friends, family and relatives), that you are not to be disturbed during study time. Make explicit arrangements regarding this issue. Generally these wishes are respected by friends and the family. See to it that you indeed study during this time. You must follow the rules that you have made for yourself.

5.1.3.1 Curb distractors

Be wary of others who misuse your time. In case there are constant interruptions, from certain friends, relatives or neighbors who consistently interrupt your efforts to study, make it clear to them in uncertain terms that your are not to be disturbed. Sometimes people do not realize that they are disturbing you when they come to visit you.

5.1.3.2 Learn to say 'no'

It may seem rude to say 'no', but, you can be courteous, polite and firm in your reply.

5.1.4 The study environment

Ensure that the study area has:

1) Good lighting
2) Ventilation
3) A comfortable table and chair to work

Ensure that the study area does not have

1) A TV
2) Loud stereo
3) A window with a view (people walking to and fro can be distracting to the eye)

You cannot concentrate on your study if the TV or stereo is on. Some people feel that they can listen to music while studying, but they only fool themselves. Silence is the best form of music for study.

5.1.5 Fatigue—Physical and Mental

In spite of tackling internal and external distractions you may still feel frequently tired. When you feel tired physically or mentally, you will not be able to concentrate.

Physical fatigue can be due to a poor diet or bad eating habits. Make it a habit to :

1) Eat regularly and
2) Eat food that is healthy and nourishing

Mental fatigue can be handled by doing exercises and yoga. This:

1) Improves blood circulation
2) Creates a good appetite and
3) Keeps the mind and body alert

Mental fatigue may be due to lack of sleep or too much sleeping, both of which are not conducive to learning. A regular day–night rhythm should be nurtured.

5.1.6 When you get stuck

1) Pay attention to work being done on hand
2) Always fragment the work to be done into manageable parts. Completion of one task will encourage you to proceed with the next.
3) Do not set vague study times, like the "whole of Sunday morning". Be specific about the time. Use a time manager (refer to the handout on time management).
4) Set a reachable study goal. Do not, for example set a goal like, "all of chapter four." Instead choose a section of the chapter or a topic in the chapter.
5) When you have worked for a long time and feel frustrated, or you realize your attention is wandering, take a break. Do not be harsh on yourself.
6) Perfection is necessary. But even this should not be taken to an extreme.
7) At the end of the day, try to finish the odd jobs that need to be completed. Tie up loose ends. The work for the next day would be that much lesser.

IS THAT ALL PRITHVI? I KNOW WHAT YOU ARE ATTEMPTING IS DIFFICULT...

Unit 6 A

Prithvi Just H(ear)s

Keywords

1. Active listening
2. Passive listening
3. Attentive listening
4. Interactive listening
5. Verbal communication
6. Non-verbal communication

Prithvi attended his new classes as a student. It was in fact very difficult the first few days to re-orient himself to this new system. It was agreed upon that Prithvi would attend classes for three hours and then continue to do his work as usual. He could work on the practical sessions whenever he was free or after office hours. There were constant interruptions.

He could not give his undivided attention to class when he still had his obligations to the office. Every now and then the phone would ring and he had to answer the caller. Visitors would come to enquire about new classes. The stationer would arrive to supply material. This was quite distracting to the instructor too. He took the matter to the proprictor and said that Prithivi would not bc ablc to lcarn anything if he were to attend to other work as well. That put an end to the problem.

Prithvi could now listen in class without external distractions. Still, there were other problems. He could not understand and follow the lecture. When the instructor asked questions in class, he could not answer them. He felt ashamed at the fact that he could not answer questions. At times, it was because he did not understand. At times, it was because he could not express himself well in English. He began to feel anxious to attend classes out of the fear that he would be unable to answer the questions.

He tried to get help from the other students. But, they were quite indifferent to him. They always treated him with a snobbish sense of condescension. They didn't listen to most lectures and made fun of those who did. They had come to have a good time, and to collect a long list of diplomas in computer courses because it was fashionable. For some, it was the third or fourth course, but ironically, they didn't even know some of the basics of computer operation that Prithvi with practical experience and intellectual curiosity had learnt.

At times, they kept interrupting the class with questions that Prithvi's attention got easily disrupted. He lost track of the direction of the lecture. And during the classes of lecturers, whom they felt were not 'good', they did not bother to listen. They passed around notes to each other, planning outings or complaining on how the class was boring.

Prithvi, however, was of the opinion that he could learn something out of each class if he listened. Mithra often used to tell him that humility, and the urge to learn were the basic requisites of the learning process. Prithvi felt so too.

The instructor who noticed this defensive attitude of Prithvi called him out of class to talk to him. Prithvi told him about his problems.

"Is that all Prithvi? I know what you are attempting is difficult. But, I am sure that a boy like you will be able to meet these challenges. Listening is not a passive experience. Your problem is more due to a lack of knowing the language. It is a problem of bad listening habits, which you can get rid of with a little effort. There is a difference between listening and hearing. Let me ask you to do a small exercise to prove my point. . ."

Prithvi collected his things, as he got ready to leave that evening. It was nearly eight o'clock. He heard a voice outside—it was a girl's voice, young, fresh and unguarded. She had come to enquire about some classes, and the peon was coaxing her to come the next day. Prithvi wondered if he could just ignore her query and go home. He was tired after the long day's work. Answering her query would mean that he had to open Room 0-8, open the cupboard, search for the prospectus and application and answer a lot of questions—it would take at least twenty minutes. The proprietor had given explicit instructions that enquiries should be attended to immediately. Besides, he knew that if he did not answer her, he would feel guilty and uncomfortable at not doing his duty.

Manasa wanted to do a summer course at the institute before college re-opened. He felt an unreasonable antipathy towards well-dressed girls who seemed to be confident about themselves. Whenever he saw a pretty girl standing in one of those beautifully built houses, he frowned at her and went by with his shoulders hunched up as if he were cold. He had never known such girls or heard them talk or seen the inside of the houses that they lived. But, he believed them all to be artificial and in a sense perverted and cunning. It took Prithvi half an hour to give her the details she required and when he reached home it was 9.00 p.m.

Self-appraisal

1. Why does Prithvi find it difficult to listen?
2. What is your opinion about Prithvi's classmates and the way they listen?

Unit 6 B

How to Be an Effective Listener

"The jungle speaks to me because I know how to listen."

—Mowgli in The Jungle Book (1994)

6.1 How much do you really listen

Statistics indicate that the normal, untrained listener is likely to understand and retain only about 30 percent of a conversation. This relatively poor percentage drops to an even less impressive 15 percent retention rate 48 hours later. This means that recall of particular lecturer will usually be inaccurate and incomplete.

6.2 Three Pitfalls of Listening

Listeners tend to run into three pitfalls that hinder effective listening. First, many think that talking is an active role and listening is a passive role. Second, people tend to over-prepare for what they are going to say and to use their listening time waiting for their next turn to speak. While anticipating for their next chance, they may miss vital information. Third, all listeners have emotional filters or blinders that prevent them from hearing what they do not want to hear.

6.3 Attentive listening and interactive listening

There are two major types of listening skills, attentive listening and interactive listening.

6.3.1 Attentive Listening Skills

Effective listening does not come easily. It involves hard work. The following attention skills will help you receive the true message the lecturer is trying to convey.

6.3.1.1 Be motivated to listen

The person with the most information has the best outcome in a class. The more you can learn, the better you will be. The real challenge comes when you need to motivate yourself to listen to someone you do not like.

6.3.1.2 If you must speak, ask questions

The goal is to get more specific and better refined information. To do so, you will have to continue questioning yourself as you listen. Your questioning sequence will be moving from the broad to the narrow and from the general to the specific. The second reason to continue asking questions is that it will help you uncover the lecturer's trend of thought.

6.3.1.3 Be alert to non-verbal cues

Although it is critical to listen to what is being said, it is equally important to understand the attitudes and motives behind the words. The lecturer may raise his voice to emphasise certain concepts. His body language may provide you cues to the understanding of certain concepts.

6.3.1.4 Listen to other's speaking

Even when you listen to your friends during a discussion in class, let the speaker tell his or her story first. Many people have learned the value of this advice from the school of hard knocks. A candidate who attended an interview for the post of a computer engineer had tried to impress the prospective employer by saying that he had specialized in Windows '98. The employer, not really familiar with computers, then told the candidate that he would not be taking him because his office had computers with Windows'95. The candidate replied that he obviously was familiar with the Windows'95 environment. But the employer had already made his decision. Had the candidate let the employer speak first, he would have been able to tailor his presentation to satisfy the employer's needs and wants.

6.3.1.5 Interrupting is rude

Do not interrupt when another student is speaking. Interrupting a speaker is not good for two reasons. First, it is rude. Second, you may be cutting off the speaker's trend of thoughts. Consequently, valuable information that may be of importance to you may be lost. Even if another student is saying something that is inaccurate, let him or her finish.

6.3.1.6 Create listening environment

Fight off distractions. When you are speaking, try to create a situation in which you can think clearly and avoid interruptions. If you can, create a good listening environment.

6.3.1.7 Noting is invaluable

Do not trust your memory. Write everything down. Any time someone tells you something in a discussion, write it down. Writing things down may take a few minutes longer, but the results are well worth the time. You will earn a tremendous amount of credibility and power as a listener.

6.3.1.8 Head for a goal

Listen with a goal in mind. If you have a listening goal, you can look for words and non-verbal cues that add to the information you are seeking.

6.3.1.9 Maintain eye contact

Give the lecturer your undivided attention. It is important to look at the lecturer in the eye when he or she is speaking. The lecturer needs to think that you are listening to him or her in class and may be able to help you by reading your body language. For instance, the blank expression on your face may persuade him to repeat concepts that you find difficult.

6.3.1.10 React

React to the message, not to the person.

6.3.1.11 Control anger

Don't get angry.

6.3.1.12 Speak or listen

Remember, it is impossible to listen and speak at the same time.

6.3.2 Interactive Listening Skills

The second type of listening skills are those used to interact with other students. These skills help ensure that you understand what the student is communicating, especially in class discussions and presentations.

Interactive skills include, clarifying, verifying and reflection.

6.3.2.1 Clarifying

Clarifying is using facilitative questions to clarify information, get additional information, and explore all sides of an issue.

Examples:

"Can you clarify this?"

"What specific information do you want?"

"When do you want the report?"

6.3.2.2 Verifying

Verifying is paraphrasing the speaker's words to ensure understanding and to check meaning and interpretation with him or her.

Examples:

"As I understand it, your idea is. . ."

"It sounds like you're saying. . ."

"This is what you've decided and the reasons are. . ."

6.3.2.3 Reflection

Reflecting is making empathetic remarks that acknowledge the other individual's feelings. This is particularly true of class seminars and presentations. If listeners are to create win/win outcomes, they must be empathetic. Most students think of themselves as relatively empathetic. In fact, most of us easily feel empathy is a skill, not a memory.

Listeners who have developed the ability to empathize can display it even when encountering speakers with whom they have little in common. The ability of a listener to empathize has been found to significantly affect the speaker's behavior and attitude. To be empathetic, one needs to accurately perceive the content of the message. Second, one has to give attention to the emotional components and the unexpressed core meanings of the message. Finally, while attending to the feelings of the other, one has to remain detached. A sympathetic individual would adopt those feelings as his or her own. Empathy involves understanding and relating to another person's feelings.

Examples:

"I can see that you were frustrated because. . ."

"You felt that you didn't get a fair treatment."

To truly practice reflective listening, you must make no judgements and pass along no opinions or provide any solutions. You simply acknowledge the sender's emotional content.

If your reflective response is constructed properly, the natural reaction from the other individual will be to provide more explanation and information.

6.4 Some key points you will find helpful in learning to be empathetic

6.4.1 Tag emotions

Recognize and identify emotions. Most inexperienced listeners are not adept at recognizing the myriad emotions. You will find it easier to identify the emotions of others if you can easily identify your own. Are you frustrated, stressed, angry, happy, sad or nervous?

6.4.2 Rephrase

Rephrase the content. If you restate the speaker's comments word for word, he or she will believe you are parroting him or her. Doing so not only sounds awkward, it will make the speaker angry. The key is to restate the content using different words.

6.4.3 Be politically correct

Make noncommittal responses.

Example: A good way to start reflective statements is with such phrases as

"It sounds like. . ."

"It appears that. . ."

"It seems like. . ."

These phrases work well because they are noncommittal. If you blatantly state, "You are angry because. . ." most people will proceed to tell you why you are incorrect.

6.4.4 Channelize

Make educated guesses when you have to talk about something that you are not familiar with. When you want to improve you listening skills, a good rule to remember is that God gave you two ears and one mouth—you should use them in their respective proportions. To understand in class, you must hear. To hear, you must listen.

THE INSTRUCTOR HAD A LOOK AT HIS NOTE BOOK AND BURST INTO LAUGHTER.

Unit 7 A

Taking Notes and Making Notes–Prithvi Learns the Difference

Keywords

1. Comprehension	3. Abbreviation	5. Overview
2. Retention	4. Signal Words	6. Emphasis

Prithvi came determined to the next class to listen actively as his instructor had told him. He tried to focus on every word the instructor uttered and take down everything he said. Of course this was difficult. It was like a race between the teacher and his pen as he wrote in a tremendous hurry trying to get at every word. He neither looked to the right nor the left nor even at his teacher. He looked only at his book. After all, he could do only one thing at a time. He could either listen or take notes.

At the end of three hours, he did not remember a word of what the teacher had said. He looked at his notes. They were so illegible and disjointed that they made no sense.

He tried to get help from the other students. But, most of them did not make notes during class. They generally felt they could always refer to books in the library or guides and get the material related to the topic. After all, they said, the lecturer only collated ideas from various books and presented it in class. When Prithvi did manage to get the note books of a few of them, their notes did not mean anything at all.

"Prithvi," the instructor called him, "Can I have a word with you?"

Prithivi stayed back in class as the others sauntered along in indolent apathy out of the class. "What were you doing in class today Prithvi?" he asked. He assumed that Prithvi had been doing some other work in spite of the fact that he had taken the trouble to talk to him the previous day. Prithvi hadn't even looked up once in his direction throughout the session. He was in fact, a little angry.

"But, Sir, I was taking notes," he said indignantly. The instructor had a look at his book and burst into laughter.

"Prithvi, this is not what I meant when I said that you should listen in class. You have misunderstood my point Listening actively, does not mean that you take down every thing that I say. I laughed just now, because, you have taken down the same point four times. I repeated the point twice for emphasis. And when two other students asked questions about the same issue I explained it to them again. You see, you were so intent on taking notes that you didn't even realize that you were doing this." Prithvi took one look at the book and had a laugh at his own mistake.

"Do you see a change in your attitude Prithvi? A week ago, if I had pointed a mistake you did, you would have sulked. But, now you are able to laugh at it. You can still learn. Try to listen first to what I say. Write the key words and ideas. Then when you go back home write the elaborate version of the notes. I think that most students in your class don't take notes. I was just looking today at the first few rows. They were taking notes in loose sheets of papers, old diaries, used up note books for school and what not. One boy even had a note book which looked so decorative and had a colourful background. That would be quite distracting to study, actually. I think you can have a look at Manasa's note book. She seems to be on the right track. And try some of the techniques I told you. If none of it works get back to me again. May be, it would help you to have a look at the notes of some of the other students who do it right."

Prithvi tried to read in advance the topic to be taught in the class. This really helped, because he could not follow what the instructor said. He wrote down all the key words, the technical terms and their meanings. He also had a look at Manasa's notebook, which she gave quite generously, and she seemed to be a nice person after all.

Self-appraisal

1. Comment on Prithvi's note taking methods?
2. What is the change in Prithvi that the instructor appreciates?
3. How would you explain Prithvi's animosity towards Manasa?

Unit 7 B

Effective Note-taking

"I have never let my schooling interfere with my education" —*Mark Twain (1835–1910)*

7.1 Lecture notes–ready made reference material

Lecture styles vary from lecturer to lecturer. Some lecturers give very detailed notes as they teach. Some lecturers are well organized and make very difficult subjects seem simple. Some make simple concepts appear difficult. Some lecturers expect the student to listen, understand and then write notes. Some give the basic outline of the subject and expect the learner to work in-depth on his own to enhance his knowledge of the subject as it very often happens at the undergraduate and postgraduate levels of study. Effective note-taking is linked with effective listening. Note-taking enhances the listening process and a systematic approach to note-taking can add immeasurably to your understanding of the course content.

7.2 Purposes of Note-taking

7.2.1 Your own tips

Taken during lectures help as learning aids towards comprehension and retention.

7.2.2 In your own hand

Notes in one's own handwriting make the material one's own. This sense of familiarity is helpful in the learning process.

7.2.3 Link to your hand

You are forced to pay attention to what is being said in order to understand and make notes.

7.2.4 Provides a map

Notes give a clear and concise outline of the most important points and ideas.

7.2.5 Points the way

They help you follow the direction of the lecture.

7.2.6 Prepares for a test

Text material supplemented by lecture notes are an excellent source of review while preparing for a test.

7.2.7 Different views summarized

Lectures often present in a ready-made package the ideas in different books by various experts. They give information on the subject that is currently developed in the field and which is not available in the text.

7.2.8 Complex to simple

They simplify complex ideas.

7.2.9 A little extra

They give extra information that is relevant or useful.

7.3 How to take notes

Frequently, students attempt to take down every word that the lecturer utters in class. This is because they do not know how to distinguish between what is important and what is not. These students have at the end of the lecture too many pages of isolated facts and details, but miss out on the more general aspect of the lecture as they are too engrossed in their attempts in writing notes.

7.3.1 Before the lecture

7.3.1.1. Tune in

Develop a positive attitude towards listening.

7.3.1.2. Preview

Read the material or text topic that is to be dealt with during the class. Reading the text prior to the class will help you.

- Get an overview of the lecture and
- Help you to decide what is important and what is irrelevant during the lecture.

7.3.1.3. Take a step back

Refer to the previous lecture notes before class.

7.3.1.4. Clarify

Look up concepts or terminology related to the class. If they are unclear, check if an explanation regarding this is given during the class. If not, ask for an explanation.

7.3.2 During the lecture

7.3.2.1 Sit up

Sit in the class where you can listen to the lecturer clearly. Do not hesitate to sit in the first row of the class.

7.3.2.2 Notebook organization

Keep a separate notebook for each subject. Writing in loose sheets of paper never works as they may get misplaced. Besides a long time will be wasted on arranging the papers than studying them.

7.3.2.3 Organize notes

Notes for each lecture should begin in a fresh page and should have details of the name of the course teacher (two or more people may teach the same subject).

- the date
- the hour or time
- the title of the topic and
- the subject code of the paper

7.3.2.4 Brevity

Your notes should be brief and should attempt to capture the main points of the topic.

7.3.2.5 Reduce

Never use a sentence when you can use a word.

7.3.2.6 Abbreviate

Use abbreviations as far as possible. Keep to standard forms of abbreviations. If you indeed want to use personalized versions of short forms, make a note of the expansion of it after the lecture when you review the notes.

7.3.2.7 As it is

However, definitions, formulae, conclusions, summaries of the topic offered by the lecturer and specific facts or data should be written exactly as spelt by the teacher. Also take down concepts that are new or ideas that you do not understand exactly.

7.3.2.8 Indent

Indent sub-points to distinguish them from main points.

7.3.2.9 Numbering

You could number your points for easier reference

For example :

I) Main Point 1

  1.1 Sub-topic 1

    1.1.1 Examples or illustrations given to prove the point

    1.1.2 Other ideas

    1.1.3 Extra information

  1.2 Sub-topic 2

    1.2.1 Examples

1.2.2 Other ideas

1.2.3 Extra information, if any

1.3 Sub-topic 3

1.4 Sub topic 4

II) Main Point 2

2.1 Sub-topic 1 and as on.

7.3.2.10 Link

The library notes you make could allude to these number at the relevant point to facilitate study.

7.3.2.11 Tracking

If notes are taken in an organized manner, you can understand the subject better and keep track of the direction of the lecture.

7.3.2.12 Coding

Develop a code to indicate the various parts of the lecture. For instance, you could have codes like these

a) imp - to refer to important topics or points in a lecture

b) * - for questions that are sure to be asked in a test

c) com - comments

d) extra - extra information

e) lib - areas where more library work has to be done

f) refer - reference to other books on the same idea made by the teacher on which you can work on later

g) ? - ideas not clear and need clarification

h) exam - assignment / test dates on the topic

Different colours can be used to refer to each of these items. Be consistent in your abbreviations. Be open minded to ideas or concepts you disagree upon.

Do not let arguing interfere with note-taking.

7.3.2.13 Questioning

Raise questions in class only if appropriate.

7.3.2.14 Clarify

Give time for the lecturer to finish the topic before you ask questions as answers to your question may be given by the end of the hour. Constant interruption, interrupts the flow of the lecture and is a distraction to the other students. Note down the issues you need clarification on and ask questions at the end.

7.3.3 After the lecture

7.3.3.1 Revise

Go through the lecture notes immediately after the lecture.

7.3.3.2 Review

Correct words or phrases that may be illegible because of the speed with which notes are taken.

7.3.3.3 Check

Check for errors in spelling of technical words (you may have taken the phonetic version of what you heard), entry of data and figures.

7.3.3.4 Clarify

Clear up any doubt at this point by consulting the teacher, the text, the other students or the library.

7.3.3.5 Fix in mind

Review the notes on the same day as you may forget the details of a lecture in about forty-eight hours (refer to the handout on Memory to the section on forgetting).

7.4 Catching Signals during Classroom Lectures

Assuming that your instructor speaks at an average speed of 120 words per minute, you would hear 6000 words in a 50 minute lecture. That's a lot of words! And that's a lot of ideas, facts, and details, too.

Lecturers use some signal words and phrases to denote:

a) the most important moments of a lecture
b) to lay emphasis or stress an idea or point
c) to impose order on a series of ideas that may seem to you to be disjointed

You will be able to organize your notes better if you focus on the use of these words. Tuning in to these words will help you discover the flow of thought and order of importance that shaped the instructor's thinking in turn, in your notes, then, you might be able to re-establish that flow and order for your own thinking.

7.4.1 Signal Words or Phrases

7.4.1.1 Example words

to illustrate   for instance   for example

The professor wants to clarify the point just made. You had better write this down or you will forget it. Write down the example even if it sounds like a narration or anecdote.

It will help you understand complex ideas better.

7.4.1.2 Time Words

prior	after	meanwhile
before	subsequently	formerly

A time relationship is being established. This answers questions like: what came first and what came last; what came in between; what came before; and what came after.

7.4.1.3 Addition Words

furthermore moreover in addition also

This seems to be an addition to the list of ideas already given. You had better write it down.

7.4.1.4 Cause and Effect Words

therefore	so	thus
as a result	accordingly	if . . . thus

This is a cause and effect word. I had better write the word effect in your notes, you can go back and write the word cause to label the preceding points.

7.4.1.5 Contrast Words

on the other hand	in contrast	conversely
pros and cons		

This is important for you to know because it gives you the other side of the picture, the research that contradicts what has already been said.

7.4.1.6 Enumeration Words

the four steps	next	finally
first, second, third, etc.		

These steps are important or the professor would not be listing them this way. You had better get them down in the same order.

7.4.1.7 Emphasis Words

more importantly	above all	remember this

This is a hint that you should remember the idea.

7.4.1.8 Repeat Words

in other words	in the vernacular	in essence
it simply means	that is	briefly

The instructor is simplifying a complex idea or simplifying a long-winded explanation. You had better make a note of this.

7.4.1.9 Swivel Words

however	nevertheless	still
yet	but	

This is a warning that there is a little bit of doubt or give-back on the point just made. You should note this qualifying remark.

7.4.1.10 Concession Words

to be sure	of course	though
granted	indeed	

These are similar to swivel words. The instructor is admitting that the opposition has a point or two. Make a note of it.

7.4.1.11 Summary Words

in a nutshell to sum up in conclusion

It is better to try and write this summary word for word: then you can study it thoroughly when you begin to review your notes.

7.4.1.12 Test Clues

this is important remember this you'll see this again

Sounds like a potential test item. It is better to try to get this down, word for word.

"THANK YOU FOR LENDING ME YOUR BOOK, MANASA."

Unit 8 A

Prithvi Finds a Remedy to Remember Well

Keywords

1. Memory	4. Mnemonics
2. Short-term memory	5. Association
3. Long-term memory	6. Acronyms

Prithvi went through Manasa's notes. They were neat and organized. One thing was surprising. She had joined a week after the course was started and yet, she was able to understand what was taught in class. While he struggled to remember the right commands for the right programmes, she was relatively at ease during the practical sessions. It must be due to her education at a good convent school, Prithvi thought. He had studied in an ordinary school. If only, he had also studied in a good school, if, he had been born elsewhere, if, he had also had educated parents like she had, if they had been rich, how much better life would have been, he wondered.

Prithvi looked at the note book. The main points were written. The sub points were indented beneath. All, he had to do was look at each point, and he could recollect all that the instructor said during the class. Prithvi made notes of several of the techniques she had used. So, that was the trick. What seemed so puzzling, now seemed so simple.

Prithvi was browsing through *The Hindu* the next morning. He watched the news in Tamil on TV regularly now. With that as a background, he tried to read through the newspaper, and could understand most of what was published. Besides, he felt the urge to know about what was happening in the world around him, something he had not bothered about earlier on.

"Thank you for lending me your book, Manasa", said Prithvi that evening. "I learnt quite a lot looking through it. Tell me one thing. How is it that you remember all that is taught in class? I always keep forgetting the commands and have to think hard to remember it. But, you are so good."

"Well, Prithvi, I am no expert. But, I have learnt a few tricks through trial and error to study better over a period of time. I also faced the kind of problems you say you have. I was never really interested in studies. My grades in my tenth standard were quite low. But, I had great dreams, I wanted to get a degree in computer engineering. Only then I realized that dreams alone don't lead us to our goals. I had to work hard for the next two years. Now, I have written my entrance exams and feel that I have done well. I may or may not get a seat. But, I am happy that I have done my best."

"I think you are right. Life is about doing our best and leaving the rest to God. I thought that I was the only one who had all the problems. I am surprised.

"Actually, most of the things I learnt come under the heading Common Sense. But, somehow we do the wrong things till we learn the right. You have to take down notes meticulously. You have to revise what has been taught from time to time. I normally use the time between classes for revising. I use a lot of flash cards or any other kind of thick card for writing key words and commands. Whenever I am free, like watching TV or late in the night when I can't concentrate well and study, I keep browsing through these cards for a change."

Prithvi was amused at what Manasa said. He thought that the only way one could remember things was to learn it by heart. Mithra's methods for remembering things was even more queer. He recollected, how as a newcomer at the hospital, he had a very difficult time, trying to remember the names of various tonics, tablets and ointments. The doctors used to say something like, "Two spoons of the pink coloured tonic in the morning, afternoon and night; one bottle of the red coloured tonic till it is over; and ten yellow capsules twice a day": This was to help the attendants pick up the right medicine. Patients often expected them to repeat the prescription of the doctor. They sometimes asked questions which they were expected to know the answers. There were problems, when the attendant gave the wrong pink coloured tonic or the wrong red capsule to the patient.

Mithra did not want this to happen to him ever. He made it a point to learn the names of all the tablets, tonic and ointments and the purposes for which they were given. He saw each tablet as a distinct personality. After a point of time the doctors preferred him to the others, because they could just give him the names of the medicine and were confident that he would take care.

He resorted to various methods to remember them, trying to associate colours with the tablets and their name, the shape of tablets and the purpose for which it is used; the rhyme, rhythm, and the phonological sounds of the name of tablets – to remember them. He learnt to pronounce the name of each tablet or tonic correctly. He repeated to himself the name of any new tablet several times till he was absolutely sure. The doctors soon saw that he was intelligent and treated him with respect. Some of the newly joined doctors were at times amazed at how he could remember the names of medicine which, even they had to think twice to remember. One young doctor used to say, "Mithra, if we have any doubts we can always come to you. When I open my own nursing home, you will be the first I would ask, to work for me. In turn, I will take care of everything you need."

And Mithra would reply in a light tone, "What is it that you can give me that I don't already have and what is it that you can offer me that I could possibly want. I am quite happy where I am."

It had been difficult for him to train himself to learn. But it gave him a great deal of pride and satisfaction at the fact that he was doing the job assigned to him with perfection. Prithvi felt that he had a lot to learn from Mithra.

Self-appraisal

1. Why do you think Prithvi finds it difficult to remember what is taught in class?
2. Do you think that the methods Manasa uses will work?
3. Mithra says that he learnt to remember the names of tablets and tonic through the process of association. Can you give an example of this related to your own subject?

Unit 8 B

Techniques to Improve Your Memory

"Half this game is ninety percent mental."

—Yogi Berra

8.1 How much do we remember

Memory is the process of storing and retrieving information. The human memory consists of a whole range of processes, from the short-term storage of sensory information, as things are perceived, to the process of retaining information for a life time.

Short-term memory is the system used to remember information "in use," such as a telephone number while you are dialing it, it is limited in storage capacity: most people can repeat a 7 or 8 digit telephone number, but not 10 or 11 digits.

Long-term memory is like a permanent personal library of knowledge, ideas and experiences—the knowledge of languages, the recollection of a personal experience or the acquisition of certain skills.

While short-term memory is limited, long-term memory appears to be unlimited! The process of moving information from short-term to long-term memory involves encoding the information in a manner that, one is able to retrieve or recall the right information at the right time.

8.2 Some useful strategies for improving long-term memory

Techniques for improving your memory
to study better and remember better

S.No	Your memory process	Technique suggested
1.	Information that is received needs to be processed and made available to the consciousness in order to transfer Short-Term Memory to Long-Term Memory.	Pay attention. The reason you don't recall the names of half the people you meet is that you weren't really listening when you were told their names. The same applies to the classroom too. Pay attention in class and make notes.
2.	The more deeply processed material is, the more likely that you will remember it for a longer period of time.	Review about the material – Think about the implications, connotations and connections, other ways of expressing the ideas. Processing the material deeply will enhance memory.

3.	Material which relates to something which you have already learnt will be easier to learn and remember than material which is totally new.	Don't try to learn material that you do not understand. Find a way of making sense of it; and then you can assimilate it. Try to relate it to material you have already learnt if possible. If it's material that can be viewed in different ways, think about how you're likely to have to recall it, and choose a method that is appropriate to that recall.
4.	All the material cannot be learnt completely.	Be selective. Choose the material which is important and focus on it in detail.
5.	Material which is repeatedly presented is more likely to be remembered. On the other hand, repetition without conscious involvement will not help.	Go over you material again and again – but not mindlessly without concentration.
6.	Material which is structured and categorized is easier to recall.	Structure and categorize all the material: make lists, draw diagrams, construct tables. Use all your senses. Visualise the material.

7.	Material which is related to yourself, or which is organized and encoded by yourself, will be remembered well.	Think about how the information applies to you. Make up your own mnemonics: make up your own lists, diagrams, tables.
8.	Experts who practice these techniques meticulously remember better.	The harder you work, the easier it gets. This is ancient knowledge: all the Vedas have come down to us from generation to generation by word of mouth through practice.
9.	Distributed practice on a regular basis is better than massed practice.	Start early, plan your study time, do a moderate amount of material each day, take breaks. Allot at least, three slots of time for study everyday and fix a standard time. Studying regularly will become a habit.
10.	A positive attitude and faith in yourself helps you to remember.	Intend to remember.

8.3 Four ways to convert short-to long-term memory

It is important to review notes from time to time as you may forget what you have studied. It has been proved that forgetting occurs very quickly. An important part of learning is "moving" information from your short-term memory into your long-term memory. Four ways to accomplish are:

8.3.1 Grouping Information

To group information is to organize it so that details are brought together under the main idea or category that connects them.

8.3.2 Visualizing Information

To visualize information is to see an image or picture of it in your mind's eye.

8.3.3 Repeating Information

To repeat information is to put the information in your own words and go over it. Say it aloud to yourself so that you can hear it as well as speak it.

8.4.4 Choosing To Remember

The more you choose to remember, the more you will remember. To choose to remember, you must pay attention to and be interested in what you are learning.

"OKAY I WILL GIVE YOU A FEW TIPS ON READING A TEXT BOOK..."

Unit 9 A

Prithvi Sees the Text in Context

Keywords

1. Highlighting	3. Scanning	5. Index
2. Skimming	4. Glossary	6. Preface

The instructors of the computer institute developed a personal interest in Prithvi and helped him in all ways possible. They encouraged him to have discussions with them whenever he was free. Prithvi for his part, made every effort to learn English. He felt that if he learned the language better, he would be able to understand concepts better. He found that proficiency in the language was a pre-requisite to reading the textbooks in the library.

There was a difference in the kind of language used in the class by the teacher and the language used in the text books. These books were quite difficult to understand. Very often, he did not even know if the topic he wanted was covered in the book. It was difficult for him to judge whether a book was really useful or relevant in the context of his course. He waded through the thick volumes of books in the hope that, if he read them with concentration, he would comprehend the text.

He now used colored cards to add any new word in the books he had learnt, and had collected something of a small database for his reference. Manasa forced him to speak in English with her. He was bashful that he would make mistakes and she would say, "Isn't it better for you to make mistakes in front of me and get corrected than make mistakes before others and feel ashamed. Only if you make mistakes and learn from them, do you learn a new skill." As a fourteen year old, she had tried to learn cycling from her cousin. At the end of the day the cousin asked if she had ever fallen during the course of the day, when she tried to cycle around. She had said with pride, "I was very careful. I didn't fall even once." At which he willfully pushed her, from the cycle and when she fell down, he said "You have to learn how to fall down too". Of course, she had been very furious with him at that moment, but, never after that had she the fear of losing balance and falling off the bike.

"Prithvi", Manasa suddenly asked, "did you see the *Titanic*?"

"Of course, I did, It was fabulous."

"Well, I didn't. Can you just tell me the outline of the story?"

"Of course I can."

Prithvi was able to narrate scene by scene the entire movie that Manasa almost had the feeling that she had seen the movie herself.

"You see, Prithvi, you are able to remember a movie that goes on for three hours at a stretch, which you saw only once, and it was an English movie too. What is it that made you remember the whole story line? Your motivation and the interest you have towards the film. You seem to remember the story of novels that you've read a long time back. You even remember many lines from novels. You read it again and again without satiation. If you can show some proportion of that interest in text books, don't you think you can read books better?

"But, Manasa, you are so unfair. How can you compare novels and movies to textbooks?"

"I agree, Prithvi. But, that is how I trained myself to get an interest in reading technical and scientific material. I had to force myself to concentrate at the beginning, but now, I have developed an interest towards reading such material. When my father used to read Francis Bacon or Arnold Toynbee, I used to wonder how he could read such stuff which was drab. But, now, I realize that it actually isn't so. Prose can be interesting."

"So, what do I do?

"Okay, I will give you a few tips on reading a textbook. You have to first skim the text, look out for the main ideas by reading the first and the last paragraph. Then look out for other ways in which the text has been organized. Then, you have to scan the text, running your eyes down the page looking out for key words and phrases. Go through the index and locate the topic you want. Once you get hold of the topic you want, you can work on it with a little more detail."

"Let me try this out with this book and I will tell you how I fare with the reading."

Prithvi was looking out at the sky. A girlish moon swept through the sky with a host of stars. Manasa had insisted on coming home that evening. She made herself at home even though his house was so hot and dingy. Prithvi's mother liked her too. And as she left, she invited Prithvi to come to her house during the weekend.

Self-appraisal

1. Why does Prithvi find it difficult to read a textbook ?
2. What do you feel about the suggestions given by Manasa to read a text book? Do you think they will work ?
3. Why does Prithvi sound appreciative of Manasa when she comes home?

Unit 9 B

How to Use a Textbook

"The covers of this book are too far apart."

—Ambrose Bierce (1842 – 1914)

9.1 The text book—the foundation of the learning process

Every new academic year opens new avenues for the student as he reads new subjects and new books. As a student in school, you might remember how you cherished the new books purchased for the academic year and how covering and labeling of these books was done with all the solemnity of a tea ceremony. You might have even tried to read the text in advance, especially the stories in the English textbooks.

As you progress to pursue higher education, this interest still persists, but, the complexity of the texts are now greater. When you try to read a text, you feel discouraged soon, because the meaning of the text eludes your comprehension. In fact, any book can be understood if you approach it the right way. Effective understanding depends on effective reading. Just as active listening is required in note-taking during lectures, so too active reading is required when reading a textbook.

9.2 The purpose of reading a textbook

The objectives in reading a textbook are:

a) to understand the material
b) to identify the main points and the supporting detail (you can't possibly memorise the entire text)
c) to learn the material
d) to produce a summary of the material for future reference

You can see that there are some similarities to our objectives in note-taking in a lecture.

9.3 The highlighting method

You could use a marker or highlighter to accentuate the main ideas and key words. Some people do not like to mark on the text. But even if a highlighter is used, it should be used sparingly.

9.4 The marginal notes method

Notes could be written in the margin area of the text. As with highlighting, be sparing in your use of cues. Use abbreviations and codes to highlight main points.

9.5 Steps for effective reading:

9.5.1 Step One—read the Preface

a) Choose a time when you are mentally fresh.

b) Read through the preface. It will give you details about the objective of the book and the way the book has been organized.

c) It also gives you a feel of the author.

9.5.2 Step Two—read the Introduction

The introduction gives a clear overview of the text, the purpose of the book, the direction it will take, a broad outline of the topics covered.

9.5.3 Step Three—look at the Table of Contents

Study the table of contents to get a general sense of the book's structure; use it as you would a road map before taking a trip.

9.5.4 Step Four—look at the Index

Check the index for the range of subjects covered or the list of authors quoted. When you see terms listed that seem crucial, look up the passage.

9.5.5 Step Five—look at the Glossary

The glossary will alert you to the new terms and concepts and their usage. When you locate a new term, try to find its definition. If you are not able to figure out the meaning, then look it up in the glossary or dictionary.

If your text does not have a glossary, it is a good idea to keep a glossary of your own in the front page of the book.

Record the terms and their definition or the page number where the definition is located.

9.5.6 Step Six—skim through the text

Spend a few minutes skimming through

a) the chapter headings
b) the main headings and
c) the sub-headings

Notice each boldface heading and subheading. And then skim through

d) each chapter
e) the diagrams, graphs or supportive pictures and
f) tables.

Notice reading aids like

g) italics
h) bold face print
i) end-of-chapter questions

9.5.7 Step Seven—read the chapters

a) Read a section at a time thoroughly and thoughtfully, aiming for full comprehension – use a dictionary to find the meaning of unfamiliar words.
b) Try to arrive at the general subject matter and its organization.
c) If you are reading the text after the lecture on the subject, try to relate the two.
d) If there are questions given at the end of each section of the text, try to answer them. They give you a clear

indication as to whether you have understood what you have learnt. Besides this, they ensure that the reading process is an active one and that it involves your total concentration on the work on hand.

e) The reading process should not be a passive one. Write notes as you read. Draw a flow chart indicating the progression of the ideas. Support the notes with visual aids such as diagrams, pictures and so on.

9.5.8 Step Eight—recite what you have read

Once you have read the text, re-read the notes that you have written and recite aloud the summary or the main ideas and the supporting details. This helps to consolidate the learning and makes the knowledge your own.

9.5.9 Step Nine—review the text from time to time

a) Review your notes frequently, along with the text on a set schedule. Often this only requires about fifteen minutes here and there during the day (or at the end of the day).

b) Frequent review helps retain your understanding and knowledge. It transports the material from short-term memory to long-term memory, one that is retentive for a life time.

c) Continuous reviewing also helps prepare you for new material and helps you to keep up a high interest level in your classes.

HIS MOTHER GAVE HIM CURIOUS STARES...

Unit 10 A

Can Prithvi Write the Report

Keywords

1.Research	3. Editing	5. Collate
2.Outline	4. Proof reading	6. Consolidate

The dead line for the assignment was nearing. There was hardly a week's time. When the instructor first announced the date of submission a fortnight ago, it sounded so far away – fifteen days time! That's a long way off, Prithvi had thought. He worked leisurely at the library and had collected sufficient material.

The assignment tested the students' ability to put to practice all that had been taught in class. They had to choose any subject of interest, collect a database and generate a report. Prithvi tried to list the work to be done into small parts and proceeded to work on it. Manasa had opted to work on the pay roll structure of a small organization.

Prithvi decided to work on the mark statement that was generated by their own firm. The present mark statement that was issued was not very reliable and it had to be checked at every point of time till the final galley was printed. Several details had to be entered manually. Though it was meant to be automatically generated by the computer, half the work was done by the firm. There were a lot of errors in the programme, which had been written at the inception of the firm, about ten years ago, and had not been updated.

Prithvi first set about doing a little survey by collecting sample mark statements and programmes from different organizations. He wrote several small programmes and tried to locate the logical fallacies behind the earlier version. However much he tried, there was some problem and it somehow did not work out right.

Getting the programme right became a sort of obsession for Prithvi. He kept thinking about the programme as he was walking home, as he was doing other work, as he travelled home and late into the night. He discussed with the instructors some of the aspects of the programme and asked for suggestions. At times, he would get up at two o'clock in the night to jot down ideas that occurred to him. His mother gave him curious stares as she saw him scribbling away at a terrific speed throughout the evening.

Gradually, he was able to locate the errors in the earlier version. As he located each error he rectified them. He had to rewrite that whole programme at times. He would stare at what he had written for hours and would be unable to locate the mistake he had made. After a point of time, he abandoned the earlier version and set about writing a new one on his own and that proved to be successful. Prithvi looked with joy, at the first few sample mark sheets. His programme worked!

The next ordeal was to write the assignment, the part he dreaded most. Again, it was the problem with his language. He had the right ideas, the accurate facts and forceful arguments, but it was a formidable task to put it on paper. Prithvi set about writing the outline of the paper, consolidating the material he had gathered from the library adding to it, his own experience and research. He was not satisfied with the rough draft. He asked Manasa to read the assignment and she offered a few suggestions and made corrections in his language.

The report was finally ready about two days before the date of submission. The instructors congratulated him on going through his report and the programme was tested and found to be a success. The proprietor called Prithvi to his room and congratulated him on his effort and success. He was very happy at the fact that he had made the right decision when he offered him the course. He said that he had some wonderful plans for him once he finished the course. Could he make a presentation of the programme and its usage to the administrative staff and faculty? Prithvi's programme was to be used with immediate effect.

Prithvi's heart sank: An oral presentation? It was all right to write an assignment or even a test. But, speaking in front of a group was different. How was he going to do it?

Self-appraisal

1. What are the problems that Prithvi has to face in writing the report?
2. What do you think made Prithvi write the programme successfully?
3. Why do you think Prithvi is afraid to speak?

Unit 10 B

How to Write an Assignment

"A scholar who cherishes the love of comfort is not fit to be deemed a scholar." —*Lao Tzu*

10.1 Writing—a cultivable skill

The task of writing seems formidable to some students. They think that writing is a gift accorded only to a few. But this is not true. Writing is a skill that can be developed with practice. By following a systematic procedure and certain ground rules you can write assignments with ease.

10.2 The purpose of assignments

The purpose of assignments or research papers is to measure a student's ability to:

1) read intelligently from several sources on a particular subject
2) pick out and organize the ideas projected therein
3) consolidate and collate the ideas
4) present them in a logical and lucid sequence

5) evaluate the material
6) arrive at conclusions about the questions you have raised or discussed in the paper.

10.3 How to write an assignment

10.3.1 Step One — Choosing the topic/subject

The topic should be specific. An assignment can cover only one major issue or topic. If the assignment topic is too general, the paper will have no focus. Read through the text and select an area of interest. Good assignments revolve around questions to which the paper attempts to provide answers. There could be a basic premise or argument, a thesis, followed by an antithesis and concluded by a synthesis.

This means that the topic should be substantial enough and amenable to growth in terms of your premise or contention.

10.3.2 Step Two — Finding sources

10.3.2.1 Limitations

It is better to refer to material that is not dated (more than twenty years old). Read the standard authors on the topic first and then move on to other writers. Read the latest essay or book on the topic if it is available. First exhaust the material in your own library and then think of other sources.

10.3.2.2 Preparing a checklist for sources

1) Consult the card catalogue in the library to locate books. It is easier than trying to browse through the whole section or shelf.

2) Use flash cards to write the details about the book you have referred to and write an abstract of the essential details. The flash card should contain details of :

a) the subject
b) the author
c) the title of the book
d) facts of publication
e) the date of publication
f) library call number

Use the standard bibliographic format to record these details.

3) Arrange the cards alphabetically and refer to them whenever required.

10.3.3 Step Three — Writing notes

a) Examine the books and articles – Skim through your sources, locating the useful material, then make good notes of it, including quotes and information for footnotes. Write the notes of each author in separate sheets. If you use a note book to write notes, make notes from a particular book as one continuum.

b) Take care in note-taking; be accurate and honest. Be sure that you do not distort the author's intended meaning.

c) Get the right kind of material.

10.3.4 Step Four — Gathering the notes

a) Examine the books and articles – several volumes at a time will save steps.

b) Skim through your sources, locating the useful material, then make good notes of it, including quotes and information for footnotes. You do not want to have to go back to these sources again. Make these notes on separate cards for each author identifying them by author.

c) Remember that you do not want to collect only those things that will support your thesis, ignoring other facts or opinions. The reader wants to know other sides of the question.

d) Get facts, not just opinions.

e) Compare the facts that you have collected from various sources and then arrive at conclusions.

10.3.5 Step Five — Writing the outline

A. Once the material has been collected, do not hurry into writing.

Ask yourself these questions:

a) What is the subject on the paper?

b) What is the purpose of the paper?

B. The outline of the essay can be indicated as below:

I Introduction

II The main text of the essay

1.1 Point One

1.1.1 Example 1

1.1.2 Example 2

1.2 Point Two

1.2.1 Example 1

1.2.2 Example 2

III Conclusion

C. Prepare an overall framework of the essay.

D. Check if the essay has coherence and a clear structure.

10.3.6 Step Six — Writing the rough draft

a) The rough draft can now be written

b) Write the paper around the outline that you have created.

c) Your introduction should state the purpose of the essay.

d) The main text of the essay.

e) Summarize what you have said.

f) Avoid long-winded sentences

g) Do not change the idea in the middle of a paragraph.

10.3.7 Step Seven — Assignment layout

a) The layout of the assignment should look neat and visually pleasing.

b) The margin space should be sufficient enough to facilitate easy reading. It should not be too little or too much.

c) Paragraphs should be spaced in a balanced manner.

d) Important lines or key ideas have to be highlighted.

Look at these two sample layouts

Sample One
is dull, with no visual focus ineffective use of margins, the topic has not been underlined or highlighted it is too crowded single line spacing, making it difficult to read.

Sample Two
has clear visual focus, enough margin space allotted, the topic stands prominent and catches the eye, visually pleasing double line spacing that facilitates readability, important lines have been highlighted.

SAMPLE ONE

SAMPLE TWO

10.3.8 Step Eight — Editing and proof reading

a) The first draft can now be polished.

b) Try to read the essay objectively and critically.

c) It would be advisable to read it at least two or three days after writing the first draft.

d) Read the paper aloud to check if there is continuity.

e) Proof read for spelling errors
f) Check the sentence construction phrasing and grammar.
g) Check if the format of the footnotes and quotations are correct.
h) Quotations should serve a purpose and not just be used. They should
    - Prove or support the idea you have expressed.
    - Illustrate and throw light upon the idea you have stated.
    - Add emphasis to your argument.

10.3.9 Step Nine — Writing the bibliography and footnotes

10.3.9.1 Footnotes

Footnotes are an important part of any essay. Whenever you borrow an idea from an author, you have to acknowledge it. Failing to do so would be plagiarism, an intellectual theft. Laws of copyright forbid this kind of misuse and a person who publishes the ideas and the words of another person and calls it his own is liable to prosecution.

Footnotes are a means to acknowledge the source of the idea and give the author the credit for the idea or concept. The idea borrowed from an author may be in agreement of disagreement with the argument of your assignment. You may quote an author to support your views or to elaborate point you have just made. The following is the standard international format for footnotes. The footnote should have the details of:

a) The author's name – the family name is always written first followed by the first name.

b) The title should be underlined and in bold.

c) The edition should be mentioned, if applicable.

d) The page number or numbers from which the lines were taken must be mentioned.

Example:

1. Smith, Susan. **Communications in Nursing**, first edition, p. 75.
2. Burton, Gwendolyn R. W. **Microbiology for the Health Sciences**, third edition, pp. 86–88.

10.3.9.2 Selected Bibliography

The bibliography is a listing of the books that you have referred to in the process of doing the assignment. This again is a method of acknowledging the sources from which ideas have been borrowed. It is also an evidence of the amount of work you have put in to do the assignment. It is 'Selected Bibliography' because you cannot list all the books that you have referred to, especially if it is a lengthy project. Some books that you refer to may not have a direct bearing on the assignment or project and may have been of marginal interest to you.

The format to write the selected bibliography is as follows:

a) The author's family name followed by a comma, followed by his first name, followed by a full stop.

b) The title of the book comes next – this should be

underlined and bold, followed by a comma.

c) The edition, followed by a comma.

d) The place of publication, followed by a comma.

e) The publisher's name followed by a comma.

f) The year of publication, followed by a full stop.

Example:

1. Smith, Susan. **Communications in Nursing**, first edition, Toronto, Mc Graw-Hill Ryerson Limited, 1986.
2. Potter, Patricia A. and Perry, Anne G. **Basic Nursing – Theory and Practice**, first edition, St. Louis, The C.V. Mosby Company.
3. Clayton, Bruce D. and Stock, Yvonne N. **Basic Pharmacology for Nurses**, ninth edition, St. Louis, The C.V. Mosby Company.

10.3.10 Step ten — The fair draft

Allot ample time for writing the fair draft. If the paper had to be typed or processed in a computer, allot at least a day for this.

Writing essays can be an interesting experience.

IT WAS JUST AS HE HAD IMAGINED...

Unit 11 A

Prithvi Has to Talk

Keywords

1. Prepare	3. Practice	5. Audience
2. Eye contact	4. Speaking anxiety	6. Extempore

Prithvi set out to Manasa's house on Saturday. It was one of these long weekends coupled with a holiday on Friday. Normally, he would have been very relaxed and happy, but the thought that he had to make a presentation on Monday made him queasy. And now, he had to go to Manasa's home. She had insisted on his coming, in spite of his refusal.

He could easily locate her house. It was just as he had imagined, a palatial house, with a Benz and Zen parked in the front to add to the general effect. The watchman at the gate kept him waiting for about ten minutes. Prithvi almost decided to leave. Just then, Manasa came running out. She apologized profusely for having kept him waiting. Her father had arrived from Dubai only the previous evening. The whole house was in a state of commotion and the watchman had forgotten her instructions.

"In that case, I will leave," said Prithvi, "wouldn't you like to spend time with your father. He is visiting you after a long time, isn't he?"

"But wait, what has that got to do with you coming home? I would like you to meet my father. I was telling him about you and he is eager to meet you."

Manasa's father was not the kind of person he had imagined. He was a very friendly person who he thought could put anyone at ease. Prithvi found that he could relate to him quite well. They discussed several things from the recent cricket match to his job and daily routine. He wasn't for a single moment condescending or sympathetic and treated him like an equal. Prithvi soon found himself sharing with him, his dreams and aspirations "When I look at you, Prithvi," he said, "I am reminded of my own youth. I have come up in life the hard way. At least, you have Mithra, your instructors, your proprietor and now me to help you. I had no one. You are lucky and you will do well."

Over lunch Manasa kept teasing Prithvi about the presentation on Monday and how nervous he was. How was he going to achieve big goals in life if he couldn't even talk about something he had created?

"I am sure you will do well Prithvi." Assured her father. "You have an interesting way of saying things that I think is a natural talent, that you are not aware of. I remember how I was when I was asked to talk for the first time. The college cultural secretary could not make it to the programme and I had to compere the whole show instead of him. The other boys refused. They were even more nervous than me, you know, boys six foot tall and hefty, back benchers who used to make a lot of noise in class, wouldn't volunteer to speak before a crowd. Any way, I took it up. I was very nervous at the beginning. But, as time went by I became comfortable and confident. I had rehearsed my role well several times the whole day. I hardly had time. I made a very detailed version of the whole show and was able to co-ordinate the whole programme. It turned out to be a success. After that, I was asked to compere several programmes in college and became something of an expert. The same may happen to you."

Prithvi felt quite confident after the talk with Manasa's father. They spoke about so many other things. Manasa's father was going to send some latest software from abroad and he said that Prithvi could work with Manasa on the home computer over the weekends. When he had completed the course, he advised that he should move on to learn another. Prithvi wanted to do the same. He wanted to learn more in the field of computers. He felt like a boy who has been taken to a shop full of wondrous things. All of it was his for the asking. All he had to do was wait, pick and choose everything one by one.

Self-appraisal

1. Why does Prithvi feel nervous when he is asked to give a presentation?
2. Manasa's father narrates his first experience of compering a programme. What do you think Prithvi learns from him?

Unit 11 B

Effective Public Speaking

"If you want me to speak for an hour, I am ready today. If you want me to speak for just a few minutes, it will take me a few weeks to prepare." —*Mark Twain*

11.1 Overcoming Speaking Anxiety

According to the book of lists, the fear of speaking in public is the Number 1 fear of all fears. The fear of dying is Number 7! Over forty-one percent of people have some fear or anxiety about speaking in front of groups. People who have this fear can experience all kinds of symptoms: Sweaty palms, accelerated heart rate, memory loss and even difficulty in breathing.

Some of the world's most famous speakers have freely admitted to nervousness and stage fright. Mark Twain said it best, "There are two types of speakers: those that are nervous and those that are liars."

Everyone, even experienced speakers, has some anxiety when speaking in front of a group of people. This is perfectly normal. The best way to deal with this anxiety is to first acknowledge that this fear is perfectly normal and you are not alone. To reduce your fear, you need to make sure you properly and thoroughly prepare yourself before you speak. Proper preparation and rehearsal can help to reduce this fear by about seventy-five percent. Proper breathing techniques can further reduce this fear by another fifteen percent. Your mental state accounts for the remaining ten percent.

11.1.1 Suggestions to reduce speech anxiety

Below are just a few suggestions you should use to overcome your speaking anxiety.

11.1.1.1 Know the room

Become familiar with the place in which you will speak. Arrive early and walk around the room including the speaking area. Stand at the lectern, speak into the microphone. Walk around where the audience will be seated. Walk from where you will be seated to the place where you will be speaking.

11.1.1.2 Know the audience

If possible, greet some of the audience as they arrive and chat with them. It is easier to speak to a group of friends than to a group of strangers.

11.1.1.3 Know your material

If you are not familiar with your material or are uncomfortable with it, your nervousness will increase. Practice your speech or presentation and revise it until you can present it with ease.

11.1.1.4 Learn how to relax

You can ease tension by doing exercises. Sit comfortably with your back straight. Breathe slowly, hold your breath for four or five seconds, then slowly exhale. To relax your facial muscles, open your mouth and eyes wide, then close them tightly.

11.1.1.5 Visualize yourself speaking

Imagine yourself walking confidently to the lectern as the audience applauds. Imagine yourself speaking, your voice loud, clear and assured. When you visualize yourself as successful, you will be successful.

11.1.1.6 Realize people want you to succeed

All audience want speakers to be interesting, stimulating, informative and entertaining. They want you to succeed – not fail.

11.1.1.7 Don't apologize for being nervous

Most of the time your nervousness does not show at all. If you don't say anything about it, nobody will notice. If you mention your nervousness or apologize for any problems you think you have with your speech, you'll only be calling attention to it. Had you remained silent, your listeners may not have noticed at all.

11.1.1.8 Concentrate on your message—Not the audience

Your nervous feelings will dissipate if you focus your attention away from your anxieties and concentrate only on your message and your audience, not yourself.

11.1.1.9 Turn nervousness into positive energy

The same nervous energy that causes stage fright can be an asset to you. Harness it, and transform it into vitality and enthusiasm.

11.1.1.10 Gain experience

Experience builds confidence, which is the key to effective speaking. Most beginners find their anxieties decrease after each speech they give.

11.2 Elements of an Effective Speech

Anyone can give a speech. Not everyone can give an effective speech. Here are six elements of an effective presentation:

11.2.1 Be prepared

Being prepared is by far the most important element.

11.2.2 Give examples

Use personal examples and experiences in your speech whenever possible. Make sure they help to emphasize or support your point. The stories must match your message.

11.2.3 The opening

Practice the opening of your speech and plan exactly how you will say it. The audience will judge you in the first thirty seconds they see you.

11.2.4 Gestures

Gestures should be kept to the minimum. Stand in a related position, feet slightly apart. Be comfortable with the stance you choose. Do not hide behind the lectern. Maintain eye contact with the audience.

11.3 Step One – Collecting material

11.3.1

Collect and read as much as material as you can about your subject.

11.3.2

Make notes.

11.3.3

Select the material that is to be presented during the talk. This depends on how long the presentation is going to be.

11.4 Step Two – Audience analysis

11.4.1

Analyze the audience you are going to address the presentation to:

A nalysis–Who are they? How many will be there?
U nderstanding–What is their knowledge of the subject?
D emographics–What is their age, educational background?
I nterest–Why are they there? Who asked them to be there?
E nvironment–Where will I stand? Can they all see & hear me?
N eeds–What are their needs? What are your needs as the speaker?
C ustomized–What specific needs should you address?
E xpectations–What do they expect to learn from you?

11.5 Step Three – Preparing an outline

The sequence of your presentation can follow one of these organizational patterns.

11.5.1 Sequential

11.5.2 Categorical

11.5.3 Problem and solution

11.5.4 Contrast and comparison

In developing the sequence of your presentation, mind-mapping or webbing techniques can be very useful. Remember to decide, too, on the transitions between sections and examples you will use. Real-life anecdotes and personal experience can be particularly effective.

11.6 Step Four – The Preparation Process

A speech needs time to grow. Prepare for weeks. Sleep on you topic, dream about it and let your ideas sink into your subconscious. Ask yourself questions. Write down your thoughts. Keep adding new ideas. Aim not only to inform your listeners, but also persuade them. As you prepare the outline ask yourself these questions.

11.6.1

In one concise sentence, what is the purpose of this speech? Let your purpose drive your speech.

11.6.2

Who is the audience? What is their main interest in this topic?

11.6.3

What do I really know and believe about this topic as it relates to this audience?

11.6.4

What additional research can I do?

11.6.5

What are the main points of this presentation?

11.6.6

What supporting information and stories can I use to support each of my main points?

11.6.7

What visual aids, if any, do I need?

11.6.8

Do I have an effective opening-attention grabber?

11.6.9

In my final summary, how will I plan to tell them "What's In It For Me?"

11.6.10

Have I polished and prepared the language and words I will use?

11.6.11

Have I taken care of the little details that will help me speak more confidently?

11.6.12

Have I given it an interesting title?

11.7 Step Five – Handling the question—and—answer session

Many presentations are followed up with a question-and-answer period. To some people this can be the most exciting part of the presentation. To others it can be their worst nightmare.

11.7.1

Listen to the entire question before you begin to answer any questions. Too many people start responding to a question before the entire question is even asked. Not waiting to hear the entire question can result in your providing a response which had nothing to do with the question.

11.7.2

Pause and allow yourself time to value the question and listener. Repeat the question aloud so that the entire audience can hear it. It is important that everyone "hear" the question or the answer you provide may not make sense to some of the people. Also, repeating the question, allows you some additional time to evaluate the question and formulate a response.

11.7.3

Credit the person for asking the question. You may say something like, "That was a good question" or, "Glad you asked that question". One word of caution. If you credit one person with asking a question, be sure to credit everyone for asking a question. You don't want people to feel their question was not as important.

11.7.4

Respond to the question honestly. If you do not know an answer to a question, do not try to fake it. Be honest, and tell them you do not know but do promise to research the answer for them and do get back to them.

11.7.5

Bridge to the next question by asking them a question. "Does that answer your question?," "Is that the kind of information you were looking for?." This is critical. Once they respond to you, "Yes" you now have permission to go on to the next person. This also gives them one more opportunity to say, "No" and allow them to clarify their question more by asking it again.

11.7.6

Ask people to stand up when they ask a question. This does two things:

11.7.6.1

It make it easier for the audience to also hear the question, and

11.7.6.2

You are able to see the person who is asking the question

11.8 Some tips on oral presentations

11.8.1 Memory aids

a) Prepare the speech in terms of a list of cues for you to remember the progression of ideas.

b) Number the visual aids and make cross references as to where they should be displayed in your list of cues.

11.8.2 Impromptu or Extempore Speaking

While many of us do not like to speak in front of people, there are times when we are asked to get up and say a few words about someone or a topic when we have not planned on saying anything at all. We are more shocked than anyone else. Below are some tips you can use the next time you are called on to speak.

11.8.2.1

Be prepared to rise to the challenge.

11.8.2.2

Decide quickly what your one message will be – keep in mind you have not been asked to give a speech but to make some impromptu remarks.

11.8.2.3

Pick one message or comment and focus on that one main idea. Many times, other ideas may come to you after you start speaking. If this happens, go with the flow and trust your instincts.

11.8.2.4

Do not try and memorize what you will say – trying to memorize will only make you more nervous and you will find yourself thinking more about the words and not about the message.

11.8.2.5

Start off strong and with confidence – if you at least plan your opening statement, this will get you started on the right foot. After all, just like with any formal speech, getting started is the most difficult. Plan what your first sentence will be. You may even write this opening line down on your note card and glance at it one more time just before you begin speaking. If you know you have three points or ideas to say, just start off simple by saying, "I would just like to talk about three points". The first point is . . . . the second point is . . . and so on.

11.8.2.6

Finally, have a good conclusion–just state, "And the last point I would like to make is . . . ." Once you have made your last point, you can then turn control back to the person who asked you to speak in the first place.

11.8.3 Things to remember

The nine P's to be remembered in an oral presentation.

Prior Proper Preparation
Prevents Poor Performance of the
Person Putting on the Presentation

He who fails to prepare is preparing for failure–so Prepare, Prepare, Prepare.

THE PROPRIETOR KEPT HIS WORD AND OFFERED HIM THE JOB HE HAD PROMISED.

Unit 12 A

Prithvi Faces the Final Test

Keywords

1. Test anxiety	4. Preparation
2. Objective tests	5. Question words
3. Multiple choice tests	6. Answer script

Prithvi's oral presentation proved to be a success. He was appreciated by all the administrative staff and faculty. There were a lot of questions asked at the end of the presentation and he was able to answer every one of them well. The programme was after all, his baby. He felt happy that he was able to give something in return to the proprietor who had given him the opportunity, which many boys in the same position might not have had.

The exams were nearing with its whole gamut of written and practical test. He had gained a lot of confidence and prepared well. He took the exams very seriously, though his proprietor had already promised him a job in the same firm as a faculty for the beginners. This relieved him of quite a bit of the tension, but, he was worried at the same time, that this may subconsciously make him complacent and nonchalant. For the same reason, he put in twice the effort he normally would have. He wanted to prove his worth and wanted to be given the job purely on merit, and not because of a sympathetic review of his background.

He looked at several of the previous question papers. He prepared model answers to questions and studied them, worked out the practical side of the test on the machine as well. He had to work late in the nights and get up quite early in the mornings. All he could see was the exams and his aim to perform well.

He had got into a kind of a fighting attitude. He remembered how as a boy, he used to observe with morbid attraction the eagle as it hovers in the sky, waiting to attack his prey. The innocent chicken would chuckle around oblivious to danger, assured of the protective safety of the mother hen. At an opportune moment, the eagle would glide swiftly down — all he could see was the swift sweep, the sharp talons, the unforgiving grasp — and it would to be over in a second. A pure struggle for survival, the will to live. Animals were unlike men. No scratching of the head, no indecision, no dubious rationalizing — all instinct and reflex, alert as a trigger. He needed to develop something of that eagle in life, though in a more positive sense, for if he failed to compete, he would be left behind.

The results, of course, turned out to be very good. Prithvi topped the class with a huge margin. The proprietor kept his word and offered him the job he had promised.

Prithvi still rushes to the office in the mornings, now, to teach boys like him. He keeps constantly updating his knowledge. He earns a very good salary every month, but spends most of it on books and software. He visits Mithra everyday. Manasa is still his best fried. She writes frequently and scolds Prithvi for not responding to her letters promptly. But, Prithvi is very busy and comes home late in the night after work. She and her mother have joined her father who is now in the US. When her father offered to get him a job abroad, he refused. He somehow couldn't leave.

Prithvi looked at the boy who had come for the interview for the post of attendant at the office. He was bright and full of dreams, and had just finished his Plus Two with very good grades. His name was Alok.

Self-appraisal

1. How does Prithvi prepare for the test?
2. Do you think that Prithvi's story of success can actually happen in real life?

Unit 12 B

Writing test successfully

"There is a country in Europe where multiple choice tests are illegal." —*Sigfried Hulzer*

12.1 The purpose of tests

Tests are tools to measure your comprehension of the course content. Very often tests are determinants of your entry into higher education, your prospects for employment and your future. The first criterion to do well in a test is, of course, your solid grasp of the course material. It also requires a knowledge of certain test-taking skills, a purposeful positive attitude and strategic thinking and planning.

12.1.1 Ability

Tests are designed to determine your intellectual and memory skills and your ability:

- to remember specific facts.
- to compare, contrast and interpret the material taught.
- to apply principles and theories taught to practical use.

- to predict possible outcomes given a set of variables.
- to discuss an issue on a broad, general manner as well as apply it in a specific context.

Test anxiety arises out of various reasons – sufficient preparation may not have been done: lack of confidence in oneself, bad time management or lack of memory. Test anxiety can be handled easily by following these strategies. Writing a test will no longer be an ordeal you have to face. Instead, it will be an opportunity to exhibit your knowledge and understanding of the subject on hand.

What to do before, during and after the test

12.2 Before the test

12.2.1 Step One — Ask questions

Find out answers for the following questions from the examiner.

12.2.1.1

What is the material for the test – the chapters, topics or areas covered?

12.2.1.2

Where will the topics be taken from – from the lecture notes, text or other sources?

12.2.1.3

What kind of a test will it be – essay, multiple-choice, true or false, filling blanks, short answers, etc.?

12.2.1.4

How long will the test be – the test duration?

12.2.1.5

How much will it count towards the total grades ? (Any test is important. But it is useful to get to know the weightage given to each test).

12.2.1.6

Is there any sample test or previous year question paper available with the examiner or the library?

12.2.2 Step Two — When you prepare

12.2.2.1

Read all the material you have collected.

12.2.2.2

If the examiner offers review sessions, use it effectively to clear all your doubts. Do not expect the examiner to repeat the lecture during these sessions. The purpose of review sessions is to enhance your understanding of the material.

12.2.2.3

Anticipate a list of questions from the point of view of an examiner.

12.2.2.4

Make a checklist of all the topics covered in the test.

12.2.2.5

Rank them according to their importance.

12.2.2.6

Start studying the important topics first.

12.2.2.7

Allot time for the test in your Time Manager (Refer to the handout on Time Management).

12.2.2.8

Allot time for revision.

12.2.2.9

Keep to the schedule. It is better to have extra time towards the end for revision than end up having no time to study because of bad time management.

12.2.3 Step Three — When you study

12.2.3.1

Integrate notes, text, and extra information that you have gathered from the library onto summary sheets.

12.2.3.2

Use diagrams, charts, tables and pictures to help you remember the material better.

12.2.3.3

Write a summary of each topic, main idea or concept.

12.2.4 Step Four — The day before the test

12.2.4.1

Get enough rest the night before a test and eat well-balanced meals. Avoid fasting on the day before the test as you may feel too exhausted to write the test.

12.2.5 Step Five — Just before the test

12.2.5.1

Be prepared emotionally, physically and intellectually.

12.2.5.2

Get into a "fighting" attitude, emotionally ready to do your best.

12.2.5.3

Arrive at the examination hall early enough to establish a calm and alert frame of mind.

12.2.5.4

It is better to stay away from others just before the test as they may transmit their anxiety on to you.

12.2.5.5

Be prepared with all the required materials (pen, sharpened pencils, rulers, erasers, calculators, colour pens/ pencils for highlighting and so on).

12.2.5.6

Bring a watch and pace yourself throughout the test.

12.3 During the test

12.3.1 Step One — When you arrive at the exam hall

12.3.1.1

If you have a choice regarding seating, choose a place with ample light and minimal distraction.

12.3.1.2

Focus on what you know rather than on what you do not know.

12.3.1.3

Reinforce your strengths and arrest your weaknesses.

12.3.2 Step Two — When you receive the question paper

12.3.2.1

As soon as you receive you question paper, use the back to jot down all the information you are worried you might forget. Remember first to ask whether you can write on the question paper itself as this is discouraged by a few examiners.

12.3.2.2

Preview the whole test before beginning to answer any questions.

12.3.2.3

Make sure your copy has no missing or duplicate pages. Ask the instructor to clarify any ambiguities.

12.3.2.4

Read the directions carefully.

12.3.2.5

Plan your time.

12.3.2.6

Allot the most time for the questions which offer the most marks.

12.3.2.7

Allocate time at the end to review.

12.3.3 Step Three — While doing test

12.3.3.1

Start with the easy questions to build your confidence and to gain time for the harder ones.

12.3.3.2

Answer all the questions. Put down some answer for each question, even if you must guess (unless there is negative marking).

12.3.3.3

Do not panic if you see a question you did not anticipate or prepare for. If you have studied well, you will remember something and will be able to answer the question.

12.3.3.4

Read the question as is. Avoid overanalysing or oversimplifying, or you will end up answering a question that exists only in your mind, and not on the examiner's answer scheme.

12.4 After the test

12.4.1 Step One — When you get back your paper

12.4.1.1

Check the total. Then go through the paper carefully.

12.4.1.2

The paper you receive from the examiner with its various red marks and red comments is actually a valuable catalogue of the kinds of mistakes you make and is an opportunity to correct yourself. If a careful analysis is made of the paper then mistakes can be avoided in the future.

12.4.1.3

Make a list of the kind of mistakes made. For instance, you may repeatedly misspell certain words consistently or get confused over concepts, which seem similar. Looking at your mistakes objectively will help you overcome them. Rework the answers with errors.

12.4.1.4

Find out by questioning yourself as to why a question was answered wrong. Is it because of a lack of comprehension? Did you have time to complete the paper? Was the paper more difficult than you expected? Was the answer expected straight from the text or did you have to incorporate other ideas too?

12.5 How to prepare for specific kinds of tests

12.5.1 The essay type test

12.5.1.1

An essay answer should have an introduction, the text and a conclusion.

12.5.1.2

It should be organized well.

12.5.1.3

There should be logic and sequence in the answers.

12.5.1.4

Focus on the way a question is worded.

12.5.1.5

It is advisable to begin the answer with the first sentence that refers directly to the question.

For example:

Question–Discuss the causes for hyper-myopia?

Answer–The causes for hyper-myopia are many and varied. . .

12.5.1.6

Examiners often say that, students fail to score well, because they do not understand the question well. The following is a list of terminology associated with questions.

S.No.	Key words in Questions	What do they mean?
1.	Analyse	Give both sides
2.	Causes	Give the reasons or causes
3.	Comment	Give your idea/opinion on the issue
4.	Compare	Focus on the similarities, mention differences
5.	Contrast	Focus on the differences, mention similarities.
6.	Define	Give an accurate meaning/ definition. Do not misquote

S.No.	Key words in Questions	What do they mean?
		definitions. It is better to paraphrase than misquote.
7.	Describe	Give the major characteristics in detail.
8.	Diagram	Make a chart/drawing.
9.	Discuss	Mention the points first and then give details.
10.	Effects	Give the results.
11.	Elaborate	Expand on the idea mentioned further in a detailed manner.
12.	Enumerate	Give the results.
13.	Enumerate	Give a list.
14.	Evaluate	Discuss both the positive and the negative side and then give your own opinion with proofs.
15.	Identify	Locate concepts or concepts asked about.
16.	Illustrate	Give examples, may be use a diagram.
17.	List	Give a list of points asked in the question. No details are required.
18.	Relate	Show how ideas or concepts are related to each other.

S.No.	Key words in Questions	What do they mean?
19.	State	Just give the main points or ideas without extra details.
20	Substantiate	Give facts or proof to support a statement.
21.	Summarize	Give key points with no personal opinions.

12.5.2 Objective tests

The purpose of objective tests is to test your ability to distinguish concepts, theories, ideas or facts. They measure your ability to remember facts and figures.

12.5.2.1 Step One — How to prepare

12.5.2.1.1

Focus on keywords and concepts. To identify key words ask questions What, Where, Who, When and How.

12.5.2.1.2

Give importance to topics that were stressed during lectures.

12.5.2.1.3

Think in terms of important vocabulary. Identify such words.

12.5.2.1.4

Use flash cards to write all these words, phrases, ideas and concepts.

12.5.2.1.5

Have frequent drills.

12.5.2.1.6

Precision comes with practice

12.5.2.1.7

Review your notes and check your power of retention.

12.5.2.1.8

Most important: Do not try to study the material in terms of bits and pieces of information. Always look at a concept in the context of the whole. It may not help to memorize the various nerves associated with the eye, without comprehending the way they work.

12.5.2.2 Step Two — At the test

12.5.2.2.1

You cannot just recognize the right answer. They require a level of high critical reasoning and a fine sense of discrimination.

12.5.2.2.2

Distinguish the way ideas, concepts or key words are different, and categorize the way ideas, concepts or key words are similar.

12.5.2.2.3

First, skim the question paper in a general manner.

12.5.2.2.4

Read the directions carefully. Look out for specific answering procedures. There may be time limits for various sections.

12.5.2.2.5

Check as to how the answer will be marked. For instance, there may be negative marking.

12.5.2.2.6

First answer all the questions that you know. Do not waste time on answering questions you do not know or have doubts about. When you feel, for instance, a question looks apparently simple, but is a little tricky, leave it to the end.

12.5.2.2.7

Work quickly, keep track of time limits and adjust you speed if necessary.

12.5.2.2.8

Then get back to the questions that you have left out and tackle them one by one.

There are many kinds of objective type of questions.

12.5.3 Multiple-choice questions

Multiple-choice questions are probably the most frequently asked objective questions. They consist of two parts:

1. The stem – the statement or question.
2. The choices – also known as the distracters. They are called so because they look like the right answer but they are not. There are usually four options from which you choose the one that will complete the stem statement or question.

12.5.3.1 How to answer

12.5.3.1.1

Read the stem as if it were an independent statement and try to complete the sentence. Then look at the choices given and decide on the correct answer.

12.5.3.1.2

Even if you know the right answer, read all the other choices.

12.5.3.1.3

Reasoning is very important in multiple choice tests.

12.5.3.1.4

Beware of qualifiers like not, but, except, never, always and so on.

12.5.3.1.5

If you do not know the answers for certain questions, try to make educated guesses from your memory of lectures, revision and your own notes.

12.5.3.1.6

Do not get paranoid with complicated questions (ones that say, "only a, only a and b, or only b and c" or questions which have options like "none of the above" or "all of the above"). Leave such questions to the end.

12.5.4 True or false tests

This is a popular test type. The basic feature of this test is that there is a fifty percent chance of your answer being right or wrong. Your odds are 50–50 with a 'hit or miss' possibility. Your answer is either right or wrong.

The purpose of the test is to measure your ability to evaluate the validity of a statement. They test your mastery of the subject. They also test your alertness by a mismatch of names or terms so as to check your accuracy and precision in understanding the subject.

12.5.4.1 How to answer

12.5.4.1.1

Beware of qualifiers like some, usually, frequently, never, always and so on.

12.5.4.1.2

Sentences that are worded in the negative form can be very tricky and may mislead you to choose the wrong answer.

12.5.5 Matching tests

The purpose of this test is to measure you ability to establish relationships between concepts, generally between Column A and Column B.

12.5.5.1 How to answer

12.5.5.1.1

If the number of items on both the sides match, it may be sufficient to know the answers to most questions. But, some clever test makers give a mismatch of the two columns, for instance, Column A may have ten items and Column B may have fifteen items.

12.5.5.1.2

You could begin with the lengthier column and evaluate the items in the shorter column as this would save time in browsing through a longer list.

12.5.6 Open-Book Test

This test is conducted to check your understanding of the lecture. There is a general misapprehension that open-book tests are very easy because students are allowed to refer to the book during the test.

12.5.6.1 How to answer

12.5.6.1.1

You will not have time to read through the material during the test.

12.5.6.1.2

A little preparation for this variety of test is absolutely essential.

12.5.6.1.3

Use post-it notes and markers to highlight the key concepts and terms.

12.5.6.1.4

Be familiar with the general layout of concepts or ideas or description of processes in the text.

12.5.6.1.5

Devise a method to access information quickly.

12.5.6.1.6

The answer should definitely not be lifted from the textbook. The skill tested here is your ability to apply the question to the material and to derive the answers.

Bibliography

Adams, W and Patterson. **Developing Reading Versatility**, eighth edition, N.Y., Hartcourt, 2001.

Albert, D. **Home Schooling and the Voyage of Self- Discovery: A Journey of Original Seeking**. M.A., Monroe, Common Courage Press, 2003.

Alexander, Robin. **Culture Pedagogy: International Comparisons in Primary Education**, M.A., Blackwell Publishers, 2001.

Allen, R. "**The Democratic aims of Service Learning**", *Educational Leadership*, 60 (6): pp. 51–54, 2003.

Atkinson, J .W. " **Motivational determinants of risk taking behavior**", *Psychological Review*, 64: pp. 359–72, 1957.

Awh, E., Jonides, J.Smith. E.E.,Schumacher, E.H., Koeppe, R.A and Katz, S. "**Dissociation of Storage and Rehearsal in Verbal Working Memory**", *Psychological Science*, pp. 7, 25–31, 1996.

Baddeley, A.D. **The Psychology of Memory**, N.Y., Hagerstown, Harper & Row, 1976.

Baddeley, A.D. **Human Memory: Theory and Practice**, revised edition, Hove, East Sussex, Psychology Press Ltd., 1997.

Baker, Ann, Jensen, Patricia, J and Kolb, D. **Conversational Learning: An Experiential Approach to Knowledge Creation**, CO, Westport, Quorum Books, 2002.

Bandura, A. **Self Efficacy: The Exercise of Control**, N.Y., W.H. Freeman, 1997.

Bartlett, S and Burton, Diana. **Education Studies: Essential Issues**, editions, London, Sage Publications, 2003.

Barwick, N. **Clinical Counselling in Schools: Clinical Counselling in Context**, edition, London, Routledge, Taylor and Francis Group, 2000.

Barrows, H.S. "**A Taxonomy of Problem- Based Learning Methods**", *Medical Education*, 20: pp. 481–86, 1986.

Bates, A. **Managing Technological Change: Strategies for College and University Teachers**, San Francisco, Jossey Bass Publishers, 2000.

Bauer, Susan and Wise, Jessie. **The Well Trained Mind: A Guide to Classical Education at Home**, N.Y., W.W. Horton & Company, 2004.

Benson, H. **The Relaxation Response**, N.Y., Morrow, 1975.

Billing, S.H. "**Research on K-12 School-based Service Learning**", *Phi Delta Kappan* 81 (9): pp. 658–64, 2000.

Biofield, J. **Taoism: The road to immortality**, Boulder, Shambhala Publications, 1978.

Boren, M.E. **Student Resistance: A History of the Unruly Subject**, N.Y., Routledge, 2001.

Bradley, L. **Curriculum Leadership : Beyond Boilerplate Standards**, Oxford, Scarecrow Education, 2004.

Broadbent, D.E. **Perception and Communication**, London, Oxford University Press, 1987.

Brody, Celeste, Fuller, K., Gosetti, Penny., Moscato, Susan., Nagel, Nancy., Pace, G and Schmuck, Patricia. **Gender Consciousness and Privilege**, London, Falmer Press.

Brosio, R. **Philosophical Scaffolding for the Construction of Critical Democratic Education**, N.Y., Peter Lang, 2000.

Brown, Sally, Armstrong, S and Thompson, Gail. **Motivating Students**, Birmingham, U.K., Kogan Page, 1998.

Brunstein J, C., Schultheiss, O.C. and Grassmann, R. "**Personal goals and Emotional well being: the Moderating role of Motive dispositions**", *Journal of Personality and Social Psychology*, 75: pp. 494–508, 1998.

Canfield, J and Siccone, F. **101 Ways to Develop Student Self Esteem and Responsibility: The Teacher as Coach**, in 2 Volumes, Boston, Allyn and Bacon, 1993.

Cantor, N and Fleeson, W. "**Social Intelligence and Intelligent Goal Pursuit: A Cognitive slice of Motivation**", in Spaulding. W., *Nebraska Symposium on Motivation*. edition, N.E., Lincoln, University of Nebraska Press, Vol. 41, pp. 125-79, 1994.

Campbell, Katy. **E-ffective Writing for E-Learning Environments**, Singapore, Information Science Publishing, 2004.

Carlson, D. **Leaving Safe Harbours: Toward a New Progressivism in American Education and Public Life**, N.Y., Routledge Falmer, 2002.

Charlesworth, R. "**Developmentally appropriate practices is for everyone**", *Childhood Education* 74 (5): pp. 274–82, 1998.

Chatterji, Madhabi. **Designing and Using Tools for Educational Assessment**, Boston, A & B, 2003.

Checchi, Daniele and Lucifora, C. **Education, Training and Labour Market Outcomes in Europe**, U.K., Palgrave Macmillan, 2004.

Cheng, Man-jan. **Lao Tzu : My words are very easy to understand**, C.A., Richmond, North Atlantic Books, 1981.

Child, D. **Psychology and the Teacher**, seventh edition, London, Continuum, 2004.

Coletta, A. **What's best for Kids**, N.J., Rosemont, Modern Learning Press, 1991.

Collins, S.C. and Kneale, P.E. **Study Skills for Psychology Students: A Practical Guide**, London, Arnold, 2000.

Collins, Kathleen. **Ability Profiling and School Failure: One Child's Struggle to be Seen as Competent**, N.J., Mahwah, Lawrence Erlbaum Associates, Publishers, 2003.

Collins, Janet and Cook, Deirdre. **Understanding Learning: Influences and Outcomes**, editions, London, Paul Chapman Pub. Co. and The Open University, 2001.

Cooley, C.M. **Human Nature and the Social Order**, *Charles Scribner's Sons, 1902.

Costa, A. and Kallick, Bena. **Assessment Strategies for Self-Directed Learning**, C.A., Thousand Oaks, Corwin Press, 2004.

Cottom, D. **Why Education is Useless**, Philadelphia, University of Pennysylvania Press, 2003.

Craik, F.I.M. and Watkins, M.J. "**The Role of Rehearsal in short-term memory**", *Journal of Verbal Learning and Verbal Behaviour*, pp. 12, 599–607, 1973.

Crawford, Glenda. **Managing the Adolescent Classroom: Lessons from Outstanding Teachers**, C.A., Corwin Press, 2004.

Creel, H.G **What is Taoism? And other studies in Chinese cultural history**, Chicago, The University of Chicago Press, 1970.

Cropley, A.J. "**Definitions of Creativity**", in M.A. Runco & S. Pritzker Encyclopedia of Creativity, Vol. I., editions, C.A., San Diego, Academic Press, pp. 511–24, 1999.

Datnow, Amanda and Hubbard, Lea. **Gender in Policy and Practice: Perspectives on Single—Sex and Coeducational Schooling**, N.Y., Routledge Falmer, 2002.

Davis, Martha., Shelmann, Elizabeth., and McKay, M. **The Relaxation and Stress Reduction Workbook**, C.A., Richmond, New Harbinger, 1980.

Dembo, M.H. **Applying Educational Psychology**, N.Y., Longman, 1998.

Diamond, M.C. and Hopson, J. **Magic Trees of the Mind**, N.Y., Plume, 1999.

Diehle, M & Stroebe, W. "**Productivity loss in brainstorming: Towards the Solution of a Riddle**", *Journal of Personality and Social Psychology,* 53: pp. 497–509, 1986.

Dodge, Ellen. **The Survival Guide for School Based Speech Language Pathologists**, edition, C.A., San Diego, Singular Publishing Group, Thomson Learning, 2000.

Dweck, C.S. **Self theories, Their Role in motivation, Personality, and Development**, P.A., Philadelphia, Psychology Press, 1999.

Dyer, W.W. **Your Erroneous Zones**, N.Y., Funk and Wagnalls Co., 1976.

Edwards, C. **Classroom Discipline and Management**, fourth edition, N.Y., John Wiley and Sons, 2004.

Ellis, A. and Harper, R. **A Guide to Rational Living in an Irrational World**, N.J., Englewood Cliffs, Prentice Hall Inc., 1961.

Emmons, R.A. "**Striving and feeling: Personal goals and subjective well-being**", editions, in: Gollwitzer, P.M. & Bargh, J.A., *The Psychology of Action: Linking Cognition and Motivation to Behavior*, New York, Guilford Press, pp. 313–37, 1996.

Ericksen, S.C. **Motivation for Learning: A Guide for the Teacher of the Young Adult**, M.I., Ann Arbor, The University of Michigan Press, 1974.

Fenske, R.F., Geranios, Christine., Keller, J.E., and Moore, D.E. **Early Intervention Programs: Opening the Door to Higher Education**, Washington. D.C., Eric Clearinghouse on Higher Education and George Washington University, 1997.

Firestone, W., Schorr, Roberta and Monfils, Lora . **The Ambiguity of Teaching to the Test: Standards, Assessment and Educational Reform**, editions, N.J., Mahwah, Lawrence Erlbaum Associates, Publishers, 2004.

Flanagan, Dawn., Ortiz, S., Alfonso,V and Mascolo, Jennifer. **The Achievement Test Desk Reference: Comprehensive Assessment and Learning Disabilities**, Boston, Allyn and Bacon, 2002.

Flavell, J.H. "**Metacognitive Aspects of Problem Solving**", edition, in L.B.Resnick, *The Nature of Intelligence*, N.J., Hillsdale, Erlbaum, 1976.

Gardner, H. **Creating Minds**, edition, New York, Basic Books, 1993.

Garner, Ruth. **Hanging Out: Community Based After-School Programs for Children**, edition, C.O., Westport, Bergin and Garvey, 2002.

Genick, Patricia. **Independent Learning and Literacy: Strategies for Elementary Teachers**, Boston, Allyn and Bacon, 1997.

Ginsberg, M and Gorastiaga, J. **Limitations and Possibilities of Dialogue among Researchers, Policy Makers and Practitioners: International Perspectives on the Field of Education**, editions, N.Y., Routledge Falmer, 2003.

Glasser, W. **Positive Addiction**, N.Y., Harper and Row, 1976.

Goldstein, E.B. **Sensation and Perception**, third edition, C.A., Belmont, Wadsworth, 1989.

Gollwitzer, P.M. "**Action phases and mind-sets**", editions, Vol. 2, pp. 53–92, in Higgins, E.T. and Sorrentino E.M., *Handbook of Motivation and Cognition: Foundations of Social Behavior*, New York, Guilford Press, 1990.

Gollwitzer, P.M. "**Implementation intentions: Strong effects of simple plans**", *American Psychologist*, 54: pp. 493–503, 1999.

Gollwitzer, P.M. and G. Oettingen, "**Psychology of Motivations and actions**", editions in chief, in Vol. 15 pp. 10105–10116, *International Encyclopedia of the Social and Behavioral Sciences,* in 25 Vols., Smelser, Neil. J. and Baltes, Paul. B., U.K., Oxford- Elsevier Science Ltd., 2001.

Greenleaf, R.K. "**Motion and Emotion**", *Principal Leadership* 3 (9): pp. 14–19, 2003.

Greg, V. **Human Memory**,* Methuen, 1975.

Gutek, G. **Philosophical and Ideological Voices in Education**, Boston, Pearson and A & B, 2004.

Hamilton, Elizabeth. **Teacher's Strategies**, Learner's Library, P.A., Springhouse Corporation, 1987.

Hanushek, E . **The Economics of Schooling and School Quality**, edition, in 2 Vols., U.K., An Elgar Reference Collection, 2003.

Hejke, H. and Muyksen. **Education and Training in a Knowledge-Based Economy**, editions, N.Y., St. Martin's Press, 2000.

Hiatt, Liisa and Klerman, J.A. **State Monitoring of National School Lunch Program Nutritional Content**, P.A., Pittsburgh, RAND Corporation—Labor and Population, 2002.

Higgins, E.T. "**Beyond pleasure and pain**", *American Psychologist,* 52: pp. 1280–1300, 1997.

Hills, P.J. **A Dictionary of Education**, edition, London, Routledge & Kegan Paul, 1982.

Hock, Ildiko. **Test Construction and Validation**, Budapest, Akademiai Kiado, 2003.

Holt, J. and Farenga. **Teach Your Own: The John Holt Book of Homeschooling**, M.A., Perseus Publishing, 2003.

Hunter, I.M.L. **Memory: Facts and Fallacies**, *Penguin, 1957.

Irvine, S. and Kyllonen, P. **Item Generation for Test Development**, editions, N.J., Mahwah Lawrence Erlbaum Associates, Publishers, 2002.

Isaksen, S.G. **Frontiers of Creativity Research**, edition, pp. 1–26, N.Y., Buffalo, Bearly Ltd., 1987.

Jacobs, H. "**Interdisciplinary learning in your classroom**, Disney learning partnership workshop at www.Thirteen.org/edonline/concept2class/month10/index.html, 2002.

Johnson, D. and Johnson, R. **Meaningful Assessment: A Manageable and Cooperative Process**, Boston, Allyn and Bacon, 2002.

Johnson, D. and Johnson, Bonnie. **Children, Testing and Failure in American Schools**, Oxford, Rowman & Littlefield Publishers Inc., 2002.

Jones, M., Jones, B. and Hargrove, Tracy. **The Unintended Consequences of High-Stakes Testing**, N.Y., Rowman & Littlefield Publishers Inc., 2003.

Jones, V and Jones, Louise. **Comprehensive Classroom Management: Creating Communities of Support and Solving Problems**, Boston, Pearson and A & B, 2004.

Kaplan, H. **Failing Grades: *How Schools breed Frustration, Anger and Violence and How to Prevent it***, Oxford, Scarecrow Education, 2004.

Katch, Jane. **They Don't Like Me: Lessons on Bullying and teasing from a Pre school Classroom**, Boston, Beacon Press, 2003.

Kerr, Mary and Nelson, C. **Strategies for Addressing Behavior Problems in the Classroom**, fourth edition, N.J., Merril Prentice Hall, 2002.

Klatzky, R.L. **Human Memory: Structures and Processes**, second edition, San Francisco, Freeman, 1980.

Knowing What Students Know: The Science and Design of Educational Assessment, Washington D.C., Committee on the Foundations of Assessment, National Academy Press.

Kordalewski, J. **Standards in the Classroom: How teachers and students Negotiate Learning**, N.Y., Teachers College Press, 2000.

Krishnamurthi, J. **On Education**, N.Y., Hagerstown, Harper Row Publishers, 1974.

Kuhl, J. and Beckmann , J. **Volition and personality: Action versus State Orientation**, W.A. Seattle, Hogrefe and Huber, 1994.

Lau, D.C. **Lao Tzu: Tao Te Ching**, M.D., Baltimore, Penguin Books, 1963.

Lebauer, R.S. **Learn to Listen, Listen to Learn: An Advanced ESL/EFL Lecture Comprehension and Note Taking Textbook**, N.J., Enlewood Cliffs, Regents/Prentice Hall, 1988.

Lepionka, Mary. **Writing and Developing Your College Textbook**, M.A., Atlantic Path Publishing, 2003.

Lleras, M. **Investing in Human Capital: A Capital Markets Approach to Student Funding**, Cambridge, Cambridge University Press, 2004.

Levin, B.R. **Energizing Teacher Education and Professional Development with Problem-based Learning**, edition, V.A., Alexandria, Association for Supervision and Curriculum Development, 2001.

Levinson, B. **We are all Equal: Student Culture and Identity**, London, Duke University Press, 2001.

Levinson, B., Cade, Sandre, Padawer, Ana and Elvir, Ana **Ethnography and Education Policy across the Americas**, C.O., Westport, Praeger, 2002.

Levitt-Anderson, Kathryn. **Local Meaning , Global Schooling: Anthropology and World Culture Theory**, edition, N.Y., Palgrave Macmillan, 2003.

Lowe, Jane and Thomas, A. **Educating Your Child at Home**, N.Y., Continuum, 2002.

Lynch, M. and Harris, Carole. **Fostering Creativity in Children, K-8: Theory and Practice**, Boston, Allyn and Bacon, 2001.

Marx, G. **Ten Trends Educating Children for a Profoundly Different Future**, V.A., Arlington, Educational Research Series, 2000.

Maslow, A.H. **Towards a Psychology of Being**, second edition, *Van Nostrand Reinhold, 1960.

Mazurek, K., Winzer, Margaret and Majorek, C. **Education in a Global Society**, Boston, Allyn Bacon, 2000.

McClelland, D.C., *et. al.* **The Achievement Motive**, second edition, * Harvester Press, 1976.

McClelland, D. **Human Motivation**, I.L., Glenview, Scott, Foresman, 1985.

McClelland, D. "**Achievement motivation in relation to achievement-related recall, performance, and urine flow, a marker associated with release of vasopressin**", *Motivation and Emotion* 19: pp. 59–76, 1995.

McDermott, C. **Beyond the Silence**, N.H., Porstmouth, Heinemann, 1999.

McCormick, Linda., Loeb, Diane and Schiefelbusch. **Supporting Children with Communication Difficulties in Inclusive Settings: School-Based Language Intervention**, Boston, A & B, 2003.

Mead, G.H. **Mind, Self and Society: From the Standpoint of a Social Behaviorist**, Chicago, University of Chicago Press, 1934.

Mottaz, Carole. **Quality High School Curriculum for Alternative Settings**, Oxford, The Scarecrow Press Inc., 2003.

Miller, G.A. "**The Magical Number Seven, plus or minus two: some limits in our capacity for Processing Information**", *Psychological Review*, pp. 63, 81–97, 1956.

Miller, W.C. **Dealing with Stress : A Challenge for Educators**, I.N., Bloomington, Phi Delta Kappa Educational Foundation, 1979.

Mills, C., Potenza, Fremer, J. and Ward, W. **Computer-based Testing: Building the Foundation for Future Assessments**, editions, N.J., Mahwah, Lawrence Erlbaum Associates, Publishers, 2002.

Nagel, Greta K. **The Tao of Teaching: The Special Meaning of the Tao Te Ching as related to the art and pleasures of teaching**, N.Y., Donald I. Fine.Inc., 1994.

Neumann, R. **Sixties Legacy: A History of the Public Alternative Schools Movement, 1967-2001**, N.Y., Peter Lang, 2003.

Nix, M. & Slavkin, M.L. " **The effects of service learning on at risk students' self esteem, self efficacy, community ownership and curricular ownership**", *National Society for Experiential Education Quarterly* 27 (4): pp. 1–15, 2002.

Noblit, G. and Echeverria-Hatt, Beth. **The Future of Educational Studies**, N.Y., Peter Lang, 2003.

O'Connor, D.J. **An Introduction to the Philosophy of Education**, *Routledge Kegan and Paul, 1957.

Oelkers, Jurgen. **Futures of Education: Essays from an Inter Disciplinary Symposium**, edition, N.Y., Peter Lang, 2001.

Oettingen, G. "**Expectancy effects on behavior depend on self-regulatory thought**", *Social Cognition* 18: pp. 101–29, 2000.

Orfield, G. and Kornhaber, M. **Raising Standards or Raising Barriers? Inequality and High Stakes Testing in Public Education**, editions, N.Y., A Century Foundation Book, 2001.

Ozmon, H. and Craver, S. **Philosophical Foundations of Education**, seventh edition, N.J., Upper Saddle River, Merrill Prentice Hall, 2003.

Paivio, A. **Imagery and Verbal Processes**, New York, Holt Rinehart and Winston, 1971.

Pankratz, R., Petrosko. **All Children can Learn: Lessons from the Kentucky Reform Experience**, editions, San Francisco, Jossey Bass Co., 2000.

Parshall, Cynthis., Spray, Judith., Kalohn, J. and Dawey, T. **Practical Considerations in Computer-Based Testing**, N.Y., Springer, 2002.

Penn-Nabritt, Paula. **Morning- by- Morning: How We Home Schooled our African-American Sons to the Ivy League**, N.Y., Villard, 2003.

Perry, W.G. **Forms of Ethical and Intellectual Development in the College Years: A Scheme**, San Francisco, Jossey- Bass Publishers, 1998.

Pillow, Wanda. **Unfit Subjects: Educational Policy and the Teen Mother**, N.Y., Routledge Falmer, 2004.

Pintrich, P.R. and Schunk, D.H. (2002), **Motivation in Education: Theory, Research and Applications**, second edition, O.H., Columbus, Merrill Prentice Hall, 2002.

Pi Wang. **Commentary on the Lao Tzu**, Honolulu, The University Press of Hawaii, 1979.

Pring, R. **Philosophy of Education: Aims, Theory, Common Sense and Research**, N.Y., Continuum, 2004.

Ravitch, Diane. **The Language Police: How Pressure Groups Restrict What Students Learn**, N.Y., Alfred a Knopf, 2003.

Reagan, T. **Non-Western Educational Traditions: Alternative Approaches to Educational Thought and Practice**, second edition, N.J., Mahwah, Lawrence Erlbaum Associates, Publishers, 2000.

Resources for Planning the School Calendar, 2004-2005, Education Research Service, V.A., Arlington, 2004.

Reynolds, Marilyn. **I Won't Read and You Can't Make Me: Teaching Reluctant Teen Readers**, N.H., Portsmouth, Heinemann, 2004.

Richert, E. Susanne. "**Toward the Tao of giftedness**", *Roeper Review*, pp. 8, 197–204, 1986, February.

Rosenfield, Sylvia and Gravois, T. **Instructional Consultation Teams: Collaborating for Change**, N.Y., The Guilford Press, 1996.

Rudestam, K. and Read-Schoenholtz, Judith. **Handbook of Online Learning: Innovations in Higher Education and Corporate Training**, editions, London, Sage Publications, 2002.

Ryan, R.M., Sheldon, K.M., Kasser, T.M. & Deci, E. L. "**All goals are not created equal: An organismic perspective on nature of goals and their regulation**", editions, pp. 7–26, in Gollwitzer, Bargh, J.A., *The Psychology of Action: Linking Cognition and motivation to behavior,* New York, Guilford Press, 1996.

Saba, Laura and Gattis, Julie. **The McGraw Hill Home Schooling Companion**, N.Y., McGraw Hill, 2002.

Salvia, J. and Ysseldyke, J. **Assessment**, eighth edition, Boston, Houghton Mifflin Co., 2001.

Sansone, Carol and Harackiewicz. **Intrinsic and Extrinsic Motivation: The Search for Optimal Motivation and Performance**, editions, San Diego, Academic Press, 2000.

Satterly, D. **Assessment in Schools in the Series: Theory and Practice of Education**, (general edition, J. Child), second edition, Oxford, Blackwell, 1989.

Shimahara, N., Holowinsky and Clarke—Tomlinson, Saundra. **Ethnicity, Race and Nationality in Education: A Global Perspective**, editions, N.J., Mahwah, Lawrence Erlbaum Associates, Publishers, 2001.

Schine, J. "**School-based Service: Recommending Schools, Communities and Youth at the margin**", *Theory into Practice* 36 (3): pp. 170–75, 1999.

Schukar, R. "**Enhancing the Middle school curriculum through Service Learning**", *Theory into Practice* 36 (3): pp. 176–83, 1997.

Skinner, B.F. **Science and Human Behavior**, New York, Macmillan, 1953.

Skinner, B.F. **Verbal Behavior**, New York, Appleton-Century-Crofts, 1957.

Slavkin, M. **Authentic Learning: How Learning about the brain can shape the development of students**, M.D., Lanham, Scarecrow Foundation, 2004.

Smelser, Neil J. and Baltes, Paul B. **International Encyclopedia of the Social and Behavioral Sciences**, editions in chief, in 25 Vols., U.K., Oxford-Elsevier Science Ltd., 2001.

Smith, D. **Essentials of Individual Achievement Assessment**, N.Y., John Wiley and Sons Inc., 2001.

Spearitt, D. **Listening Comprehension: A Factorial Analysis**, Melbourne, Australia, A.C.E.R Books, 1962.

Stevens, M. **Kingdom of Children: Culture and Controversy in the Home Schooling Movement**, Princeton, Princeton University Press, 2002.

Taylor, S.E., Pham, L.B., Rivikin, I.D. & Armor, D.A. "**Harnessing the imagination: Mental simulation, Self-regulation, and coping**", *American Psychologist* 53: pp. 429–39, 1998.

Thorkildsen, Theresa. **Motivation and the Struggle to Learn: Responding to Fractured Experience**, Boston, Allyn and Bacon, 2002.

Thompson, Rosemary. **Crisis Intervention and Crisis Management : Strategies that Work in Schools and Communities**, N.Y., Brunner -Routledge, 2004.

Tileston, Donna Walker. **What every Teacher Should Know about Student Motivation**, C.A., Thousand Oaks, Corwin Press, 2004.

Ur, Penny. **Teaching Listening Comprehension**, Series edition, London, Cambridge University Press, 1984.

Vaughn, Sharon and Briggs, Kerri . **Reading in the Classroom: Systems for the Observation of Teaching and Learning**, edition, London, Paul Brookes Publishing Co., 2003.

Vernon, M.D. **The Psychology of Perception**,*Penguin, 1962.

Walsh, W.M. and Williams,G. **School and Family Therapy: Using Systems Theory and Family Therapy in the Resolution of School Problems**, edition, I.L., Springfield, Charles C. Thomas Publisher, Ltd., 1997.

Wall, E. **Educational Theory: Philosophical and Political Perspectives**, edition, N.Y., Prometheus Books, 2001.

Watts, A., and Huang, A.C. **Tao: The watercourse way**, New York, Pantheon, 1978.

Whitley, B. and Keith-Spiegal, Patricia. **Academic Dishonesty: An Educator's Guide**, N.J., Mahwah, Lawrence Erlabaum Associates, Publishers, 2002.

Weiner, B.J. **Human Motivation: Metaphors, Theories and Research**, London, Sage, 1992.

Weist, M., Evans, S. and Lever, Nancy. **Handbook of School Mental Health: Advancing Practice and Research**, edition, N.Y., Kluwer Academic/Plenum Publishers, 2003.

Wild, Rebecca. **Raising Curious, Creative and Confident Kids: The Pestalozzi Experiment in Child-Based Education**, Boston, Shambala, 2000.

Wolfe, P. **Brain Matters: Translating research into Classroom Practice**, V.A., Alexandria, Association for Supervision and Curriculum Development, 2001.

Wood, D. "**Problem-based Learning**", *British Medical Journal,* 326 (Feb): pp. 328–31, 2003.

Wright, R. "**Brehm's theory of motivation as a model of effort and cardiovascular response**", editions, pp. 424–53, in Gollwitzer P.M. and Bargh J.A., *The Psychology of Action: Linking Cognition and motivation to behavior*, New York, Guilford Press, 1996.

Yon, D. **Elusive Culture: Schooling, Race and Identity in Global Times**, N.Y., State University of New York Press, 2000.

Zenger, Sharon and Zenger, W.F. **57 Ways to Teach: A Quick Reference for Teachers**, C.A., Los Angeles, Crescent Publications, 1977.

Zoch, P. **Doomed to Fail: The Built-in Defects of American Education**, Chicago, Ivan. R. Dee, 2004.